The Classical Monologue
Women

Michael Earley is a literary adviser and producer for BBC Radio Drama and Senior Editor-at-Large for Methuen Drama. Formerly Chairman of the Theater Studies Program at Yale University, he has also taught dramatic literature, acting and playwriting at the Juilliard School's Drama Center in New York City, New York University and various other places in the US and UK. He has worked in professional theatre as Literary Manager for the Acting Company (US) and Princeton's McCarter Theater Company (US).

Philippa Keil is a writer and translator who holds an MFA from the Yale School of Drama (US) where she acted, directed and studied dramaturgy. She also took an undergraduate degree at the University of Sussex, where she produced plays for the Frontdoor Theatre, and then worked professionally in London at the Orange Tree Theatre.

by the same authors

Solo! Best Monologues of the 80s (Men and Women)
Soliloquy! The Shakespeare Monologues (Men and Women)

The
Classical Monologue
Women

Edited with notes and commentaries by

MICHAEL EARLEY
& PHILIPPA KEIL

Theatre Arts Books
Routledge · New York

First published as a paperback original
in Great Britain in 1992 by Methuen Drama,
7/8 Kendrick Mews, London sw7 3HG

Published in the USA in 1992 by
Routledge Theatre Arts Books, 29 West 35th Street,
New York NY 10001

A CIP catalogue record for this book
is available from the British Library
and the Library of Congress
ISBN 0 87830 033 3

Printed and bound in Great Britain
by Cox & Wyman Ltd, Reading, Berkshire

Contents

French and Spanish

Restoration and Eighteenth-Century English

English and Irish (Nineteenth and Twentieth Century)

German, Scandinavian and Russian

Acknowledgements

Grateful acknowledgement is made for permission to reprint extracts from copyrighted material to the following:

Amber Lane Press for *Phedra* translation copyright © Robert David MacDonald 1985, 1991.
Harcourt Brace Jovanovich, Inc. for *The Misanthrope* translation copyright © Richard Wilbur 1954, 1955. Methuen Drama for *Medea*, translation copyright © Jeremy Brooks 1988, from *Euripides: Plays One*; *Life is a Dream* translation copyright © Gwynne Edwards 1991, from *Calderón Plays: One*; *Woyzeck* translation copyright © 1979, 1983, 1987 by John Mackendrick, from *Büchner: The Complete Plays*.
The Society of Authors on behalf of the Bernard Shaw Estate for *Mrs Warren's Profession* and *Major Barbara* by Bernard Shaw.

Caution

Notes to the Actor

A while back when we were putting together a selection of great monologues for women from Shakespeare's plays, appropriately called *Soliloquy!*, we knew that there would eventually be a need for a companion volume that would be an anthology of a limited selection of the great stage speeches from other ages of classical drama. This is that volume. It follows the course of drama from Aeschylus to Shaw, covering major periods and styles that also reflect the great ages of classical stage acting. In putting together this volume we have at last placed Shakespeare in an appropriate context. He is still in this volume but now as one writer among many glorious companions.

During the last decade there has been an unprecedented explosion of new productions of classical plays. The classical repertoire has returned with a vengeance as fierce as some of the monologues in this volume. More young actors and directors than ever before are exploring this rich vein of tradition, unearthing dramas which have languished on dusty shelves of libraries and showing them to have a size, weight and theatricality sorely missing in most contemporary work. The classical actor now stands on a par with the contemporary one. Learning how to be a classical actor is now every bit as important as knowing how to be a modern one.

Any actor, at some point in her career, must measure herself against the greatness of a classic text. All of these works have endured through time because they are filled with the very stuff that makes drama dramatic and theatre theatrical: tension, conflict, heroism, emotionalism, risk, danger and magnitude. This last item is particularly crucial, for in doing a classic piece of theatre an actor must instantly transform and enlarge herself mentally, physically and emotionally. The text gives you the capacity to do it. Once you surrender yourself to a great piece of classic theatre writing you really become a three-dimensional performer – the speech instantly showing each and every side of you. That is why these speeches are so terrific for auditions.

There is nothing timid or puny about the speeches in this volume. Any great classic speech is a gift for an actor and the last thing you need ever worry about is the fear of being inarticulate or boring. All the speeches you will encounter here have this one feature in common and in most instances they require you to pull out all the stops. You can wrap yourself in soaring lines of verse or prose as though language were a magnificent costume. They also require a strong voice and blatant physicality. You cannot hide behind these speeches but have to use them boldly to show off your skill and daring as a performer.

There are many ways of approaching these speeches as audition pieces, but the one thing you must do above everything else is approach them imaginatively. You must use the character's needs, desires, articulateness, spirit and wilfulness as a means of expansion. You must make imaginative leaps and substitutions so that you become the character herself caught in the turmoil of struggle. Few of the speeches here are naturalistic, most of them employ heightened rhetoric and none of them are stumbling or humbling. You must use the language like a trampoline that will launch you into acrobatic flight. On-stage, the best classical dramas give actors the capacity to soar; they enable the actor to be memorable by being moving. In the end your job is to move the audience.

The various commentaries and notes that accompany these monologues consciously avoid any instructions on 'how to act' these speeches. They are there to highlight interesting features in a monologue that you might not instantly see for yourself. They are also there to help you if you get stuck or confused about a particular speech or word. We have not written a series of 'director's notes' but really just appreciations of what is good about the writing from the point of view of acting. You the actor must make your own decisions about how, ultimately, to perform any of these classical monologues. There is no one right way to act these speeches. No two actors will ever do any of these monologues in quite the same way, which accounts for the thrill and unceasing wonder of live performance.

We would be foolish, however, not to admit that many of these pieces are a genuine test and challenge of your imaginative reach. So we have tried to include pieces of varying degrees of difficulty plus characters of different ages and experiences. The actor must bring to any of them an appetite for words and a willingness to experiment and play with infinite acting possibilities. Reading these speeches silently and understanding them intellectually will not help you very much to perform them. These speeches only reveal their potency and resonances once they are lifted off the page and taken onto the stage to be released out loud. The solidity and power of great dramatic language live best when they echo in a theatre. Actors are the mediums of that release.

One last piece of crucial advice before you move on to the speeches themselves. No dramatic monologue can be satisfactorily detached and set adrift from its context within either a scene or the total play. Young actors especially, in a restless search for fresh audition material, will use isolated speeches without any familiarity of the plays from which they come. Acting does not work that way. You must see the character within the widest frame of reference – the play itself. You must read the play's full text in order to examine a character's complete needs and complex dramatic life. Before you can ever act any speech you must be certain why you, as the character, choose to say what you say now. The passion that all these speeches have in abundance requires your full engagement with the text. Acting in isolation from the total text is stilted acting, blind acting without insight.

Michael Earley
Philippa Keil
London 1991

A Word about the Translations

Except where indicated after specific texts, all translations in this volume are by the editors. At the end of the volume there is a 'Play Source' that points you to a published reading version of each script.

Agamemnon (The Oresteia)
(c. 458 BC) Aeschylus

Mycenae in Argos. In front of Agamemnon's palace

*King Agamemnon has just returned from he Trojan War with
Cassandra, a prophetess, as his captive. He . greeted by his wife
Queen Clytemnestra (30s-40s) in a tense reunion. She is planning to
murder him in revenge for his earlier sacrifice of their daughter
Iphigenia. Agamemnon and Clytemnestra enter the palace across a
royal purple cloth, and after several speeches of fear and foreboding by
the Chorus and Cassandra (who then enters the palace) we hear the
death cries of Agamemnon from within. Clytemnestra appears at the
door triumphantly standing over the dead bodies of Agamemnon and
Cassandra.*

CLYTEMNESTRA.
What words I said before suited necessity;
without the slightest shame, I now unsay them all.
Under a tender guise my hate matched his manly hate.
The trap I set for his ruin was too high to vault.
For my own part the conflict born of an ancient grudge
has been pondered long and deep.
What I planned to do, has now been done.
Here I stand where I struck him down.
He could not escape the stroke of death, nor beat it aside.
Like a fisherman casting his tightly woven net,
I snared him in a mesh of deadly crimson cloth.
I struck him twice. Twice he cried and fell to his knees.
Once down I delivered the third and final blow,
in thanksgiving to Hades, lord of the underworld,
        guardian of the dead.
So he fell, his life throbbed away;
Breath and blood spurting out of him like a shower,

spattering me like drops of crimson dew.

I soaked it up joyfully as spring buds do the gods' sweet
    rain.

It is over and done, these are the facts.

If it pleases you, noble elders of Argos, be glad.

But for me – I am triumphant.

The dead deserve libations, the sacrament of religion.

Agamemnon has the just deserts of death.

He filled our cup with such an evil brew,

he has himself now come home and drunk it to the dregs.

[lines 1372–1398]

COMMENTARY: The trilogy of tragedies that comprises Aeschylus' *Oresteia* (*Agamemnon, Libation Bearers, Eumenides*) dramatises the story of the return of King Agamemnon from the Trojan War and his death at the hands of his wife Clytemnestra and her lover Aegisthus; the revenge of her son Orestes who murders the adulterous couple; and Orestes' subsequent flight and trial. The doomed fate that hovers over the mythological House of Atreus is compounded by acts of regicide and matricide in the first two plays. Madness and fury propel the third play until a jury of Athenian citizens and the goddess Athene absolves Orestes of his guilt, ending the trilogy in concord. Like so many of Aeschylus' plays, the dialogue is written primarily as a series of lengthy monologues between a principal actor and the Chorus. The speeches are highly rhetorical and require an effectively sustained vocal stamina.

Clytemnestra addresses a Chorus of elders, displaying the dead bodies of Agamemnon and Cassandra tangled in a web of gory cloth at her feet. This is her public defence, justifying what is essentially the murder of a king. The Chorus is not instantly swayed but reacts in horror to her brutal deed, calling her evil, proud and mad. Over the many years that Agamemnon has been away waging war with Troy, Clytemnestra has been brooding on vengeance. Her bitterness stems from Agamemnon's sacrifice to the gods of their elder daughter Iphigenia in order to gain favourable winds for the Greek fleet on its way to Troy. Clytemnestra's grudge is a long-standing one and her murderous revenge takes place swiftly after Agamemnon's arrival back in Troy. Her rage is also set in motion by the appearance of Cassandra, a daughter of King Priam of Troy, whom Agamemnon has brought back to his palace as his war prize and concubine and jealousy becomes mingled with vengeance. Several speeches later she vents further rage over Cassandra's body. Notice the solid and graphic images. Clytemnestra simply describes what she did and how she did it in all its gory details. The crimson cloth is a vivid prop. It is all bluntly told without remorse, fear or sense of guilt. She seems to feel that the public justification of the act is self-evident even though her motives are wholly personal. The triumphant gloating at the end of the speech is what the Chorus finds impossible to condone.

Antigone
(*c.* 441 BC) Sophocles

Thebes. In front of Creon's palace.

Antigone (16–20) is the sister of Polynices who has been killed in his attempt to reclaim the throne of Thebes from Creon his uncle. Against Creon's orders Antigone goes to bury the slain Polynices and is caught in the act. After a scene of confrontation Creon condemns her to death in spite of the fact that her action was justified and that she is betrothed to his son Haemon. Antigone is to be sealed up and left to die in an underground cell. Here she speaks to the Chorus before she is lead away to her entombment.

ANTIGONE.
   I go to my tomb, to my bridal-chamber, to my
       everlasting prison
   carved out in the rock, there to meet with my blood kin
   who Persephone has already welcomed among the dead!
   I, the last and most miserable of them all,
   while still in the flush of youth,
   shall descend there and as I enter yield up my life.
   But I hold dear the hope that when I arrive there
   my father, my mother and my brother will welcome me.
   At each of your deaths it was I, with my own hands,
   who bathed and dressed you, who poured libations on
       your tombs.
   You, Polynices, know how I ministered to your corpse,
   and it is for that act that I am thus condemned.
   But the wise will bear witness – this ritual of honour was
       rightfully done.
   Even if I were mother and wife, with children and
       husband dead,

I would let them rot in their graves rather than break the
     laws of this city.
What law justifies these words?
A husband lost, another could be found,
and from him another child replacing the dead child.
But with my mother and my father dead there can be
no hope of producing another brother to bloom beside
     me.
This then was the law by which my action honoured you.
But, dearest brother, to Creon my action was an outrage
and a crime. And so he orders me away and by force I am
     taken.
For me there is no marriage-bed, no feasting or songs.
Thus unmarried, I have no children in need of nurture.
Still alive, sad and friendless, I go to death's vaults.
And what law of the gods have I trangressed?
Why, in my misery, would the gods even hear my plea?
Since my act of piety is condemned as impiety.
Is there any one among them who would take my side?
No, if the gods think this judgement is righteous,
Then I shall suffer this punishment and see my crime for
     what it is.
But if the crime has been done by those who judged me,
then I hope that they, in their turn, will suffer
a punishment that is equal to mine.

                                        [*lines 891–928*]

COMMENTARY: *Antigone* is the final play in Sophocles' Theban
cycle about King Oedipus. It focuses on the tragic events
unfolding from the attempted rebellion against Thebes by Polynices, Oedipus' son, who hoped to regain the kingship from
Creon his uncle. The play is an impassioned debate about
whether or not the interests of the state should prevail over family
loyalties. This is the central conflict that absorbs all the characters. The immediate action of the play focuses on Antigone's

struggle of conscience and her rebellion against Creon's strict edict forbidding the lawful rites and burial of Polynices. Although the city has been saved from civil unrest, Antigone's personal unrest becomes the highlight of the drama.

This speech is Antigone's final one in the play. The actor must approach it as though it were one long exit speech and summation. Antigone's life is being cut short. She faces certain death on the eve of her marriage, just as she is about to enter maturity as a woman. This, plus the fact that she will not bear children, becomes her primary concern. She also articulates the dramatic crux of the play: private needs versus public duty. There is nothing clear-cut in any Sophoclean monologue. A character acts and reacts out of passion and loyalty to family bloodline. One of the most challenging elements in the monologue is the consolidation of her life into past, present and the dire future to come as she is on the verge of being led away under armed guards. The actor must confront the speech as a highly personalised reaction to Antigone's situation and fate. She says nothing about her civic responsibilities (although she did earlier in the play and here seems to contradict that) or what her actions mean in terms of the common good. There is something selfish about Antigone which the actor must justify in order to give the speech credibility. Antigone has much of Oedipus' fire and pride and quite a bit of her brother's natural rebelliousness. Up to this point she was expecting to marry Haemon, Creon's son, and eventually become queen of Thebes, but her dramatic decision to honour her obligation to her own family (a major character trait) has transformed her within the space of several scenes into a radical and an outcast. One of the most dramatic elements of the speech is Antigone's realisation of what her sentence and doom entail. Here is how Creon describes her sentence just before this monologue begins: 'Away with her, away. And when you have enclosed her, according to my word, in her vaulted grave leave her alone, forlorn, whether she wishes to die or live a buried life in such a home.' She will not be put to instant death but rather undergo a slow death by physical entombment. The idea of isolation and wasting away has to prey on the character's mind.

Medea
(*c.* 431 BC) Euripides

Corinth. Before the palace of Creon.

*Medea (30s) who has come to live in Greece as the wife of Jason, the
Greek adventurer, suddenly finds that she is being cast aside because
Jason now wants to marry the daughter of King Creon of Corinth.
Medea, however, will not give him up without a fight. Here as she
addresses the Chorus she considers some of her options for vengeance.*

MEDEA.
Yes, yes, I am hemmed in on every side.
But don't imagine all my battles lost.
I can deal trouble too.
Trouble is looming for this young bride,
And for the bridegroom, a whole sea of it.
Do you think I would have fawned on that man there
Without some purpose? No, I would never
Have spoken to him, let alone touched him!
But if he had banished me today, as he intended,
My plans would have been ruined. Well, luckily
He's fool enough to grant me this one day –
Enough to devise a fate for these three enemies,
Father and daughter, and my faithless husband.
I have thought of so many ways to kill them,
My friends, I am at loss to choose.
Shall I set fire to the bridal chambers?
Or steal into the bedroom where the sheets enfold them
And plunge the sharp sword through their pumping
      hearts?
The danger there is that I might be caught
And killed myself before my sword has spoken,

Leaving the last laugh to my enemies.
No, I will not be mocked; give them no chance
To make the name Medea a laughing stock.
The simplest way is best, the way
We women are most skilled at,
The way of poison.
Well, now: suppose them dead.
What city will receive me? What host
Offer me friendly shelter, a home
And sanctuary? There's none.
I've gained a little time, so I will stay
My hand a little while, and hope to find
Some new ally to offer me a refuge.
Then I could do my murders with quiet cunning.
But if I'm banished with no hope of safety
I'll seize the sword in my own hand
Even if I die for it, and kill them,
Yes, go out boldly to the kill, and kill.
By Hecate, the fearsome Queen of the Underworld,
Whom I revere above all other gods,
Whom I have chosen as my task's accomplice,
By Hecate, the secret guest of my soul,
Not one of these shall soil my honour
And fail to pay for it.
They shall repent their marriage
In bitterness and pain; bitterly repent
Their wooing, bitterly repent my banishment.
Come then, Medea!
Plot and scheme,
Use all your magical arts,
Now comes the testing time,
Up, and on to the danger!
Remember what you have suffered and still suffer.
You cannot let this royal Corinthian house,
The race of Sisyphus, use Jason's wedding

To mock Medea, daughter of a king
Sprung of Helios the Sun-god.
You have cunning enough. Besides,
We that are born women
Though little apt for noble deeds
To fashion mischief are most expert.

[*lines 364–409*]
Translated by Jeremy Brooks

COMMENTARY: Euripides' *Medea* is one of the most theatrically
thrilling of all Greek tragedies, largely because of the oustanding
heroine at its centre. Medea, an Eastern princess who the Greeks
consider to be a barbarian outsider, betrayed her father and
homeland by sacrificing everything in order to save the life of
Jason and to help win him the fabled golden fleece. Returning to
Greece as Jason's wife and mother of their two children, she is
spurned by him as he ambitiously and openly pursues a marriage
with Creon's daughter and the wealth and standing it will bring
him. Jason is an adventurer and opportunist who will act without
honour and by deceit. Fearing that Medea will take revenge,
Creon attempts to exile her. The tragic ending of the play involves
the murder of Jason's bride, Creon and her own two children
before she is whisked from the scene in a dragon-drawn chariot.

This is one of the most powerful women's speeches in classical
Greek tragedy. The actor will instantly see that it has little to do
with honour and duty but is single-mindedly concentrated on acts
of revenge. Emotion overwhelms her reason. Medea has good
cause to feel the way she does. She is spurned by Jason for purely
technical reasons: by marrying a Greek princess the citizenship of
his two children will become legal. Euripides in this play attacks
xenophobia and attitudes to women. The playwright helps win
sympathy for Medea's cause by characterising Jason as cold and
calculating. The actor must remember that Medea is an exotic
character, an alien force among the so-called civilised Greeks. She
has used witchcraft and cunning in the past and will use them
again in the future when she produces the poisonous robes and
crown that burn her victims to death. She has much in common
with Shakespeare's Lady Macbeth in her ability to plot murder.

9

Her speech is almost an aria of fury which she delivers in heightened but controlled rage. Her anger and passion must be served by the actor. She calls upon the gods of the underworld as the speech eventually settles into incantations and conjuring. Here is where the actor must get very bold with the language and reproduce Medea's visions of vengeance which become the source of her later actions. She becomes the personification of revenge and whoever plays her must become consumed by that motivation.

Electra
(*c.* 418 BC) Sophocles

Mycenae in Argos. In front of Agamemnon's palace.

*King Agamemnon has been murdered by his wife Clytemnestra with
the aid of her lover Aegisthus. Together they now rule the kingdom.
Orestes, her son and rightful heir, has fled. Electra (16–20), the
daughter of Agamemnon and Clytemnestra, and Orestes' sister, enters
the scene and addresses the Chorus of young women. She gives a vivid
account of what her life is like under the rule of her mother's tyranny
and why she continues to mourn her father's death.*

ELECTRA.
  If it appears to you that I am constantly mourning
  and lamenting, then I am ashamed.
  I ask that you forgive me. Does not my background
  and being my father's daughter urge me
  to bear witness to all that has happened in this house?
  From day to day, from morn to night,
  this endless increase of wrongs is one ceaseless sorrow.
  The first cause is my mother. My mother hates me.
  Here in this house I must live with my father's
      murderers.
  I am subject to their rule, beholden
  to them for each and every thing I do.
  Can you imagine passing the days watching Aegisthus
  sitting on my father's throne, seeing him
  in my father's robes, witnessing him pour libations
  on the very spot where he killed my father.
  Espying the worst outrage of all, this murderer of my
      father,
  in my father's bed with her, with my mother.

As his mistress, brazenly she lives with this
foul and contaminated criminal, fearing no fury.
Far from it, she laughs in the face of what she has done.
She marks that day, the day of my father's
treacherous murder, celebrating it with song and
        sacrifice.
Every month, on that day, she gives thanks
to the gods who saved her. I must confront
the profane ceremony, that commemorates his name,
suppressing my grief and lamentation,
holding them tight inside my body.
My heart cries for tears, but I will not let them show.
And this woman, this empress of deceit, taunts me:
'What a wretched girl you are, you damnable creature,
Do you think you're the first ever to have lost a father?
Does no one else ever mourn? I curse you.
May you never find escape from your sorrows,
not even in the underworld!'
And on and on she taunts me, unless
she hears a rumour that Orestes is coming.
Then she goes mad and shrieks in my face.
'This is your fault,' she says. 'I have you to thank for
        this,
you stole him from my embrace and forced him to go
        away.
Mark my words, you will pay for this.'
By now she is screaming, and at her side
her noble lord backs her up, like the coward he is,
that type of man who picks a woman as his foe.
I must wait and wait, doing nothing.
Waiting for Orestes to return and right all our wrongs.
He always intended to do it, and so
I wait and wait, endlessly waiting,
until any scrap of hope dies with me.
How can you suggest restraint

and piety from someone in such a state?
Evil surrounds me, and I must be evil!

[lines 254–309]

COMMENTARY: *Electra* is widely considered to be one of Sophocles' most technically accomplished plays, especially in the way he brings Orestes and Electra together. The dramatic action concerns the return of Orestes and his revenge upon his faithless mother Clytemnestra and her traitorous lover Aegisthus for their cold-blooded murder of Agamemnon. The tension in the early stages of the play builds largely through the speeches of Electra. Her meeting and recognition of her brother are delayed by Sophocles until two-thirds of the way through the drama. The early parts of the action focus separately on Orestes' revenge plot and Electra's laments. At one point, Electra receives news that Orestes is dead and she resolves to take revenge on her own.

The character Electra is one of the most bracing portraits of a young woman in all of Greek drama. Her speeches are vivid, personal and almost modern (particularly in her attitude to her mother). She is angry, vengeful in spirit, yet cautious about when and how to act. She is not restrained by weakness but freely admits here that her sorrow and mourning are her inescapable duty. All the seeds of her resentment are contained in this speech which turns her into a version of a female Hamlet. The speech is full of preoccupations with time and the burden of waiting: time since the death of Agamemnon and the waiting for the return of Orestes. Electra is trapped in a holding pattern and all she can do is watch, grieve and suffer her mother's abuse. The playwright gives the character the chance finally to unleash all her pent-up feelings to the Chorus who challenge her excessive displays of sorrow. Notice how she is restrained from action. The speech girdles and contains her ('suppressing my grief and lamentations,/ holding them tight inside my body'). There is a nice piece of well-aimed mockery at the expense of her mother and Aegisthus who come to vivid life as she portrays them, especially when she imitates her mother. The actor would do well to look at the earlier dialogues between Electra and the Chorus in order to see how Sophocles builds the tensions which are finally expelled in this speech.

The Spanish Tragedy
(*c.* 1586) Thomas Kyd

Act 5, scene 2. Spain. Hieronimo's garden.

Isabella (40s) is the wife of Hieronimo, a Marshal of Spain. Her son Don Horatio was found murdered in the family garden earlier in the play. Vengeance has been slow in coming and during that time Isabella's hapless grief over her son's tragedy has gradually driven her insane. Here she strikes out with a knife in her hand, in a speech that also sees her physically ripping apart the place where Horatio's body was found hanging from a tree.

ISABELLA(*with a weapon*).
Tell me no more! – O monstrous homicides!
Since neither piety or pity moves
The king to justice or compassion,
I will revenge myself upon this place,
Where thus they murdered my belovèd son.

She cuts down the arbour.

Down with these branches and these loathsome boughs
Of this unfortunate and fatal pine!
Down with them, Isabella; rent[1] them up,
And burn the roots from whence the rest is sprung!
I will not leave a root, a stalk, a tree,
A bough, a branch, a blossom, nor a leaf,
No, not an herb within this garden-plot, –
Accursèd complot[2] of my misery!
Fruitless for ever may this garden be,

[1] **rent** cut and root
[2] **complot** accomplice
14

Barren the earth, and blissless whosoever
Imagines not to keep it unmanured![3]
An eastern wind, commixed with noisome airs,
Shall blast the plants and the young saplings;
The earth with serpents shall be pesterèd,
And passengers,[4] for fear to be infect,
Shall stand aloof, and, looking at it, tell:
'There, murdered, died the son of Isabel.'
Ay, here he died, and here I him embrace:
See, where his ghost solicits with his wounds
Revenge on her that should revenge his death.
Hieronimo, make haste to see thy son;
For sorrow and despair hath cited[5] me
To hear Horatio plead with Rhadamanth.[6]
Make haste, Hieronimo, to hold excused
Thy negligence in pursuit of their deaths,
Whose hateful wrath bereaved him of his breath.
Ah, nay, thou dost delay their deaths
Forgives the murderers of thy noble son,
And none but I bestir me – to no end!
And as I curse this tree from further fruit,
So shall my womb be cursèd for his sake;
And with this weapon will I wound the breast,
The hapless breast, that gave Horatio suck.

She stabs herself.

[*lines 1–38*]

COMMENTARY: Kyd's *The Spanish Tragedy* was one of the most popular and influential Elizabethan plays. It created a vogue for a ghoulish form of melodrama and its impact can be seen in other

[3] **unmanured** uncultivated
[4] **passengers** passers-by
[5] **cited** summoned, also incited
[6] **Rhadamanth** Radamanthus, one of the mythical judges of the underworld

famous revenge tragedies, most notably Shakespeare's *Hamlet*. It is full of ghosts, deceit and outrageous villainy. The play also employs theatrically effective scenes and characters, calculated to excite an audience. An extremely political plot, involving the rivalry between Spain and Portugal, is thrown aside after Don Horatio, Hieronimo's son, is murdered by Don Balthazar, a violent Portuguese prince, and a rival for the hand of Bel-Imperia. The death and discovery of Horatio unleash a chain of incidents that culminates in the punishment of the villains and the separate suicides of Hieronimo and his wife Isabella.

Isabella, a very minor character in the play, suddenly comes to dramatic life in this very late scene. Neither justice nor revenge has rooted out the murderers of her son, leaving her mad and in despair. So Isabella decides to take 'justice' into her own hands. With a knife as a kind of scythe she chops down the vines and branches in her arbour, the scene of her son's murder and where he was found hanging from a tree (the 'fatal pine'). Powerless to be a revenger herself (that is a role reserved for her husband Hieronimo), Isabella can only take revenge on the scene of the murder. This is an incredibly physical scene. Isabella is one of the first in a long line of Elizabethan and Jacobean madwomen who usually play scenes of madness with their hair loose to indicate the venting of emotion and lack of constraint. Her speech, in blank verse, puts into words her shock and trauma at the memory of her son's death. The brutal, macabre murder carried out at night in the garden has given the scene a weird and forbidding atmosphere. The actor should notice that Isabella expresses her grief in deeply vocalised vowels, particularly the 'o' sounds at the start: 'Tell me no more – O monstrous homicides!' Sorrow becomes a deeply felt emotion echoed in the very words themselves. The garden itself and each of the plants becomes a personified accomplice in the murder, even the very air participated in the crime. Isabella wants revenge since she cannot have justice. The most surprising aspect of the speech is her abrupt suicide at the end, unprepared for and very swift. The dramatic consequence of this scene is that it will force Hieronimo to finally revenge the murder so it must be performed with high impact.

Tamburlaine (Part 1)
(*c.* 1590) Christopher Marlowe

Act 5, scene 1. Western Asia in the fourteenth century. A military camp.

Zenocrate (20s), daughter to the Sultan of Egypt, is first the captive and then the wife of Tamburlaine, the ruthless conqueror. Tamburlaine and his troops lay siege to the city of Damascus and butcher the inhabitants. Seeing the carnage and so many of her countrymen dead, Zenocrate registers shock and dismay. She tries to reconcile what she sees with her love for Tamburlaine as she unburdens herself to her maid Anippe.

ZENOCRATE.
Wretched Zenocrate, that liv'st to see
Damascus walls dy'd with Egyptian blood,
Thy father's subjects and thy countrymen;
The streets strowed[1] with dissevered joints of men,
And wounded bodies gasping yet for life;
But most accurs'd, to see the sun-bright troop
Of heavenly virgins and unspotted maids,
Whose looks might make the angry god of arms
To break his sword and mildly treat of love,
On horsemen's lances to be hoisted up,
And guiltlessly endure a cruel death.
For every fell and stout[2] Tartarian[3] steed,
That stamp'd on others with their thund'ring hoofs,
When all their riders charg'd their quivering spears,
Began to check the ground[4] and rein themselves,

[1] **strowed** strewn
[2] **fell and stout** fierce and strong
[3] **Tartarian** i.e. referring to Tartarus, the infernal regions of hell
[4] **check the ground** i.e. stop short

Gazing upon the beauty of their looks.
Ah, Tamburlaine, wert thou the cause of this,
That term'st Zenocrate thy dearest love?
Whose lives were dearer to Zenocrate
Than her own life, or aught save thine own love.
But see, another bloody spectacle!
Ah, wretched eyes, the enemies of my heart,
How are ye glutted with these grievous objects,
And tell my soul more tales of bleeding ruth![5] . . .
Earth, cast up fountains from thy entrails,[6]
And wet thy cheeks for their untimely deaths!
Shake with their weight in sign of fear and grief!
Blush Heaven, that gave them honour at their birth
And let them die a death so barbarous.
Those that are proud of fickle empery[7]
And place their chiefest good in earthly pomp,
Behold the Turk and his great Emperess.[8]
Ah, Tamburlaine my love, sweet Tamburlaine,
That fights for sceptres and for slippery crowns,
Behold the Turk and his great Emperess.
Thou that in conduct of thy happy stars[9]
Sleep'st every night with conquest on thy brows,
And yet would'st shun the wavering turns of war,
In fear and feeling of the like distress,
Behold the Turk and his great Emperess.
Ah, mighty Jove and holy Mahomet,
Pardon my love, O pardon his contempt
Of earthly fortune and respect of pity;
And let not conquest ruthlessly pursu'd

[5] **ruth** compassion, pity
[6] **entrails** pronounced as three syllables
[7] **empery** absolute empire
[8] **Behold . . . Emperess** She refers to Bajazeth and his wife Zabina who have committed suicide just before this speech and whose bloody bodies lie on-stage.
[9] **conduct . . . stars** i.e. Tamburlaine's conquests are guided by fate.

Be equally against his life incens'd
In this great Turk and hapless Emperess.
And pardon me that was not mov'd with ruth
To see them live so long in misery!
Ah, what may chance to thee, Zenocrate?

[*lines 319–371*]

COMMENTARY: Marlowe's *Tamburlaine* is a two-part heroic tragedy that follows the rise and fall of the lowly Scythian shepherd Tamburlaine as he becomes a mighty conqueror. It is full of long speeches written in Marlowe's patented ringing blank verse. Marlowe's great contribution to the Elizabethan stage was his creation of energetic and highly individual characters whose aspirations and language mirror those of the high Renaissance. Generally his male characters (Tamburlaine, Dr Faustus and Edward II) are singled out for their great portrayals of heroism on a grand scale. Zenocrate (pronounced: *Zee-no-kra'-tee*) is one of the very few female characters to receive this same treatment.

Zenocrate's speech comes towards the end of the play and summarises much of the lamentable loss which warfare and destruction have produced. She is in love with Tamburlaine's better parts (his vision, ambition and courage) but she cannot reconcile the barbarous and bloodthirsty side of his character. Like a heroine from a Greek tragedy (a conscious imitation on Marlowe's part), she has a visionary capacity to describe scenes of violence that seem to us almost cinematic in their scope and clarity. The actor must remember that Marlowe wrote for a very confined stage with no scenery and that speeches like this were meant to enlarge the viewers' capacity in place of actual battle scenes. The delivery of Zenocrate's speech must be huge and must fill space. Although in the depths of sorrow at the sight of the 'bloody spectacle', she is very controlled and has an extremely elegant command of language and imagery. Notice that all the names give the speech a rich and exotic quality. She reproduces the horror in the form of verbal action pictures; everything is in vivid close-ups. Note the parts about limbs and horses. For the speech to have genuine impact, the actor should obey the ten-beat iambic pentameter line which Marlowe uses to great effect. It is a good idea to score the speech rhythmically so that the accents can enhance an emotional release. Four times she repeats the line 'Behold the Turk and his great Emperess.' Each time she delivers this refrain it can take the actor to a new plateau of feeling. You have to find the steps in the speech to sustain both its length and emotional progression. She concentrates on the death of the Turkish Emperor Bajazeth and his Emperess Zabina (who have dashed out their brains in the scene immediately preceding this speech) because she might see them as fateful portraits of both herself and Tamburlaine.

Arden of Feversham

(*c.* 1592) Anonymous

Act 3, scene 5. Arden's house at Feversham.

Mistress Alice (20s), the young impulsive wife of the older Thomas Arden, a wealthy gentleman of Feversham in Kent, has been having an adulterous affair with the steward Mosbie. Together they have plotted Arden's death and are in the midst of waiting to hear whether or not the murder has been carried out. Alice and Mosbie have just had an argument as their guilty fears and suspicions of each other divide them. Alice tries to convince Mosbie of her fidelity to him and seeks a reconciliation.

ALICE.
Ay, now I see, and too soon find it true,
Which often hath been told me by my friends,
That Mosbie loves me not but for my wealth,
Which too incredulous I ne'er believed.
Nay, hear me speak, Mosbie, a word or two;
I'll bite my tongue if it speak bitterly.
Look on me, Mosbie, or I'll kill myself:
Nothing shall hide me from thy stormy look.
If thou cry war, there is no peace for me;
I will do penance for offending thee,
And burn this prayer-book, where I here use
The holy word that had converted me.
See, Mosbie, I will tear away the leaves,
And all the leaves, and in this golden cover
Shall thy sweet phrases and thy letters dwell;
And thereon will I chiefly meditate,
And hold no other sect but such devotion.
Wilt thou not look? Is all thy love o'erwhelmed?

Wilt thou not hear? What malice stops thine ears?
Why speaks thou not? What silence ties thy tongue?
Thou hast been sighted[1] as the eagle is,
And heard[2] as quickly[3] as the fearful hare,
And spoke[4] as smoothly as an orator,
When I have bid thee hear or see or speak,
And art thou sensible[5] in none of these?
Weigh all thy good turns with this little fault,
And I deserve not Mosbie's muddy looks.
A fence of trouble is not thickened still:
Be clear again, I'll ne'er more trouble thee.

[*lines 113–142*]

COMMENTARY: *Arden of Feversham* is a domestic tragedy and probably the first and best example of this genre in Elizabethan drama. Rather than deal with royalty it deals with a middle-class family. The action of the play centres on the efforts of Mistress Alice Arden and her lover Mosbie to plot and execute the murder of Alice's husband Thomas Arden. The play is full of sensational twists and turns of plot, events both highly dramatic and melodramatic that threaten to turn into farce at some points. It was based on a notorious murder committed in 1551 and presages Shakespeare's *Macbeth*. In a recent revival of the play it was clearly shown that the roles are as lively and actable today as they would have been in the sixteenth century. Since the motivations of the characters come from real human needs rather than from metaphysical ones, everything they say and do has a reason and cause.

One of the great strengths of the play is the portrait of Alice Arden. She is passionate, impulsive and wholly honest about her desires and sexuality. She is also a cunning manipulator. You can see in her an early sketch for Shakespeare's Lady Macbeth.

[1] **sighted** gifted with such sight
[2] **heard** gifted with hearing
[3] **quickly** acute
[4] **spoke** gifted with speech
[5] **sensible** capable of making sense

Critics have claimed that Alice is the most lifelike character to have been depicted in English drama up to this time. Look at how simple and direct her language is as she pleads with Mosbie who has just cursed and discredited her in the most despicable terms. In her distress Alice makes use of open vowels and short syllables to echo her reaction: 'Ay, now I see, and too soon find it true . . .' The entire speech is one long plea focused on Mosbie. It is also clear that Mosbie has turned away from her physically. Everything she says is calculated to win back his attention and favour: look, listen, speak are the main impulses. They have almost a physical impact. Physical, too, is the manner in which she literally threatens to tear pages from her golden prayer-book. The passion of their sinful affair has reached that level of sacrilege. She then tries flattering him, desperately likening his prowess to that of an eagle, a hare and an orator. This seems to do the trick in winning him round. Her insinuations set the remainder of the scene on the way to reconciliation.

Richard III
(1592–4) William Shakespeare

Act 1, scene 3. London. The royal court.

Queen Margaret (50s–60s), the widow of King Henry VI and mother of the murdered Prince Edward, is addressing Queen Elizabeth, wife of the dying King Edward IV, and the assembled nobles. Margaret has become a pariah at court and has the freedom to harangue at will with unsettling taunts. Here she challenges everyone.

QUEEN MARGARET.
  What? Were you snarling all before I came,
  Ready to catch each other by the throat,
  And turn you all your hatred now on me?
  Did York's dread curse prevail so much with heaven
  That Henry's death, my lovely Edward's death,
  Their kingdom's loss, my woeful banishment,
  Should all but answer for[1] that peevish[2] brat?
  Can curses pierce the clouds and enter heaven?
  Why then give way, dull clouds, to my quick[3] curses!
  Though not by war, by surfeit[4] die your king,
  As ours by murder, to make him a king!
  Edward thy son, that now is Prince of Wales,
  For Edward our son, that was Prince of Wales,
  Die in his youth by like untimely violence!
  Thyself a queen, for me, that was a queen,
  Outlive thy glory, like my wretched self!
  Long mayst thou live to wail thy children's death

[1] **answer for** pay back, recompense
[2] **peevish** silly
[3] **quick** lively
[4] **surfeit** excessive indulgence in sensual pleasures

24

And see another, as I see thee now,
Decked[5] in thy rights, as thou art stalled[6] in mine!
Long die thy happy days before thy death,
And, after many lengthened hours of grief,
Die neither mother, wife, nor England's queen!
Rivers and Dorset, you were standers-by,
And so wast thou, Lord Hastings, when my son
Was stabbed with bloody daggers: God, I pray him,
That none of you may live his natural age,[7]
But by some unlooked[8] accident cut off!

[lines 188–214]

COMMENTARY: Shakespeare's *Richard III* covers the rise to power, the bloody rule and the fall of Richard, Duke of Gloucester (later King Richard III). It is the last in a series of plays that covers the lamentable reign of Henry VI and the civil strife of the Wars of the Roses between the feuding houses of York and Lancaster. The remnant of Lancastrian rule is represented in this play by the mad, spiteful and prophetic Queen Margaret, the widow of Henry VI. She has seen her son, Prince Edward, slaughtered in the power struggle and gleefully watches the growing dissent within the usurping house of York. She vividly likens them to a bunch of 'snarling' dogs at each other's throats. She comes in and out of the action of the play like a vengeful spirit cursing characters and events, reminding all present that they too will come to a bad end (which they all do in their own ways).

Margaret, though usually portrayed as an old woman, is one of the liveliest characters in the play. She has a major role through three plays (*Henry VI, Parts 1* to *3*) and makes her presence felt in each of her brief appearances in this one. The vivacity of the young Margaret is still apparent in the old harridan. Her function in the play is to be a fierce prophetess of the ill-fortune to come. She speaks with complete freedom every time she is on-stage and

[5] **Decked** covered
[6] **stalled** installed
[7] **natural age** full lifespan
[8] **unlooked** unexpected

this liberates the actor to take risks with the character and use her cursing words like stinging, venomous barbs. All of her lines are in balanced blank verse so the rhythm of the speech can have a mesmerising effect. It should rise up to the final threatening 'cut off!' Her speech continues further after this but the character will need time to recharge herself for the next assault of words. The names she cites are like a litany of the living and the dead. Use them to evoke her full sense of rage and threat of what is to come. Part of Margaret's strategy is to compare herself with the unfortunate Queen Elizabeth, a woman who will be a successor to Margaret's woe. So notice that all of her addresses to Elizabeth have a hammering tit-for-tat quality: 'Edward thy son . . . For Edward our son'; 'Thyself a queen for me that was a queen.' Margaret becomes the living conscience of the full cycle of the drama.

Romeo and Juliet

(*c.* 1595) William Shakespeare

Act 2, scene 5. Verona. Outside Capulet's house (possibly an orchard).

Juliet (14) is the daughter of the noble Capulets, who has met and fallen in love with Romeo, son of the Montagues. Their families are locked in an ancient, bitter feud. Their meeting and balcony scene have led to their declaration of love despite the danger of their family animosities. Juliet has sent her Nurse to Romeo at nine that morning to learn how and when they may marry. Here she eagerly awaits her Nurse's return with Romeo's reply.

JULIET.
  The clock struck nine when I did send the Nurse;
  In half an hour she promised to return.
  Perchance she cannot meet him. That's not so.
  O, she is lame! Love's heralds should be thoughts,
  Which ten times faster glide than the sun's beams
  Driving back shadows over louring[1] hills.
  Therefore do nimble-pinioned doves draw Love,[2]
  And therefore hath the wind-swift Cupid wings.
  Now is the sun upon the highmost hill
  Of this day's journey, and from nine till twelve
  Is three long hours, yet she is not come.
  Had she affections[3] and warm youthful blood,
  She would be as swift in motion as a ball;
  My words would bandy[4] her to my sweet love,

[1] **louring** menacing
[2] **nimble-pinioned . . . Love** i.e. Venus' chariot drawn by swift-winged doves
[3] **affections** passions
[4] **bandy** strike backwards and forwards, like a ball in tennis

27

And his to me.
But old folks, many feign as[5] they were dead –
Unwieldy, slow, heavy, and pale as lead.

Enter Nurse and Peter.

O God, she comes! – O honey Nurse, what news?
Hast thou met with him? Send thy man away.

[NURSE. Peter, stay at the gate. (*Exit Peter.*)]

Now, good sweet Nurse – O Lord, why lookest thou sad?
Though news be sad, yet tell them merrily;
If good, thou shamest the music of sweet news
By playing it to me with so sour a face.

[NURSE. I am aweary. Give me leave awhile.
Fie, how my bones ache! What a jaunt have I had!]

I would thou hadst my bones, and I thy news.
Nay, come I pray thee, speak, Good, good Nurse, speak.

[NURSE. Jesu, what haste! Can you not stay awhile?
Do you not see that I am out of breath?]

How art thou out of breath, when thou hast breath
To say to me that thou art out of breath?
The excuse that thou dost make in this delay
Is longer than the tale thou dost excuse.
Is thy news good or bad? Answer to that;
Say either, and I'll stay[6] the circumstance.
Let me be satisfied; is't good or bad?

[*lines 1–37*]

---

[5] **feign as** pretend as if
[6] **stay** wait for
28

COMMENTARY: Shakespeare's *Romeo and Juliet* follows the fated tragic course of a doomed love affair. Romeo and Juliet become so impassioned and blinded by love that they ignore all the dangers that their relationship and decision to marry secretly will produce. The private scenes of their exchanges of love and vows alternate with the public scenes of antagonism between the houses of Montague and Capulet. Romeo and Juliet are caught in this conflict and become the sacrificial victims whose deaths resolve the feud.

Juliet is full of unbridled expectation as to what news her Nurse will have for her. She is youthful and impulsive. There is hardly a word in her highly romantic speech of the danger that this love will breed (except for the ominous line 'Driving back shadows over louring hills.') Notice how she wants time to pass swiftly. She says this several times in different speeches in the play. Juliet is a character in a constant state of anticipation. Throughout you must physically show how delirious she is with eagerness. She is also, you will notice, impatient which makes her say mean things about her old Nurse. But when the Nurse returns she is all a-glow for news. The speech is full of antitheses, or oppositions, which add tension to the lines: suns versus shadows; sad versus sweet; swift versus slow; sweet versus sour; good versus bad. The actor should use the questions to portray Juliet's fierce insistence to get the answers she longs to hear. The blank verse is generally regular, except for abrupt irregularities and lapses, as in the half-line pause in line 15 where it comes to a sudden stop. You must decide why Juliet pauses here and how to fill the silence. You will notice that the speech speeds up and slows down and speeds up again, the shifting tempo mirroring Juliet's changing moods. See if you can work with this to give the speech variety. Juliet's excitement when the Nurse finally returns is opposed by the Nurse's being too out of breath to answer her insistent questions.

As You Like It
(1598–1600) William Shakespeare

Act 3, scene 2. Arden. The forest.

Rosalind (18–20s) has been banished from the court by her uncle Duke Frederick. Together with her cousin Celia and her clown Touchstone, she sets off disguised as a young man and finds herself in the Forest of Arden. There she finds Orlando, a man also in exile from the court and to whom she is romatically attracted. He in turn is pining for the Rosalind he believes he left behind. Unable to reveal herself and drop her disguise as Ganymede, she befriends Orlando and offers to tutor him on how to woo women. In one of these scenes of ironic courtship she launches into thoughts about the effects of love and how to cure them.

ROSALIND.
Love is merely[1] a madness and, I tell you, deserves as well a dark house and a whip as madmen do;[2] and the reason why they are not so punished and cured is that the lunacy is so ordinary that the whippers are in love too. Yet I profess curing it by counsel.

[ORLANDO. Did you ever cure any so?]

Yes, one, and in this manner. He was to imagine me his love, his mistress; and I set him every day to woo me. At which time would I, being but a moonish[3] youth, grieve, be effeminate, changeable, longing and liking, proud, fantastical, apish,[4] shallow, inconstant, full of tears, full of smiles; for every passion something and for no passion truly

---

[1] **merely** completely
[2] **dark . . . do** (a common contemporary treatment for the mad)
[3] **moonish** fickle
[4] **fantastical, apish** capricious and foolish

anything, as boys and women are for the most part cattle of this colour; would now like him, now loathe him; then entertain him, then forswear him; now weep for him, then spit at him; that I drave[5] my suitor from his mad humour[6] of love to a living humour of madness, which was to forswear the full stream of the world and to live in a nook merely monastic. And thus I cured him; and this way will I take upon me to wash your liver[7] as clean as a sound sheep's heart, that there shall not be one spot of love in't.

[ORLANDO. I would not be cured youth.]

I would cure you, if you would but call me Rosalind and come every day to my cote[8] and woo me.

COMMENTARY: Shakespeare's *As You Like It* is an irrepressibly romantic comedy with one of Shakespeare's best heroines. Rosalind, the daughter of the exiled Duke Senior, is cast out of court by the latter's usurping brother Duke Frederick. She goes in search of her father to the Forest of Arden. She adopts the disguise of a young man, Ganymede, to protect herself. The change in identity, however, causes problems when she encounters Orlando, a man passionately in love with the 'Rosalind' he met at court. She in her disguise as Ganymede sets out to cure him of his lovesickness, falling in love with him herself in the process. All is righted in the end as identities and positions sort themselves out.

Rosalind's prose speech is full of ironies. She is teaching Orlando the hard facts of wooing. Love, she is saying, is not all poetry and rhymes. It is more serious than that. More to the point Rosalind is trying to demonstrate love's power to confuse and dislocate. You cannot miss the irony that, dressed as a man, she is dislocated herself. In Rosalind's terms love is like a sickness, a 'madness'. Notice how she resembles a physician diagnosing

[5] **drave** drove
[6] **humour** disposition
[7] **liver** (thought to be the body's seat of love)
[8] **cote** cottage

symptoms and then prescribing a cure. She treats Orlando like a patient, thereby protecting herself from direct involvement in the problems of love. Her innate intelligence is greater than Orlando's and he rarely interrupts her once she launches into one of her elaborate similes. Notice how she goes on and on, before she reaches a full end-stop in a line. The speech is written as a catalogue of items and you must give a life and an emotional weight to each one of her ideas and images. Notice, too, that there is a lot of opposition, or antithesis, within the lines to create tension. You must decide how much Rosalind is saying this speech for Orlando's romantic education, and how much for her own. As dispassionate as she might seem, she herself is also in love with Orlando. Her great strength as a character, however, is that she is a realist and not a romantic. Being in disguise, she has the freedom to say what she pleases and uses it to speak in a way she never could as Rosalind.

A Woman Killed with Kindness
(1603) Thomas Heywood

Scene 13. Yorkshire. A room in Master Frankford's house.

Anne Frankford (20s) is the good wife of the kindly gentleman John Frankford. Their domestic bliss is shattered when Frankford's erstwhile friend Wendoll seduces Anne. Gradually Frankford observes their infidelity and confronts them both. Wendoll flees the scene and Anne and Frankford are left alone to confront one another. The shame of the situation is too much for them both and Frankford seems unable to berate her as an adulteress. Here she speaks to him, anticipating his rage.

ANNE (*enters in her nightgown*).
    Oh, by what word, what title, or what name,
    Shall I entreat your pardon? Pardon! Oh!
    I am as far from hoping such sweet grace,
    As Lucifer from Heaven. To call you husband –
    Oh me, most wretched! I have lost that name;
    I am no more your wife . . .
    I would I had no tongue, no ears, no eyes,
    No apprehension, no capacity.[1]
    When do you spurn me like a dog? When tread me
    Under your feet? When drag me by the hair?
    Though I deserve a thousand, thousand fold,
    More than you can inflict – yet, once my husband,
    For womanhood, to which I am a shame,
    Though once an ornament – even for His sake,
    That hath redeemed our souls, mark not my face,
    Nor hack me with your sword; but let me go
    Perfect and undeformed to my tomb!

[1] **capacity** powers of reason

I am not worthy that I should prevail
In the least suit; no, not to speak to you,
Nor look on you, nor to be in your presence;
Yet, as an abject,[2] this one suit I crave –
This granted, I am ready for my grave.

[*lines 75–103*]

COMMENTARY : The main plot of Thomas Heywood's domestic tragedy *A Woman Killed with Kindness* revolves around the duplicity of Wendoll towards his friend John Frankford ('the most perfectest man / That ever England bred a gentleman') and the eventual adultery between Wendoll and Frankford's wife Anne ('Beauty and Perfection's eldest daughter'). Gradually Frankford accepts the evidence of his wife's and friend's infidelity and punishes her not by branding her an adulteress but by tormenting her with kindness and exiling her from his sight. She eventually dies by pining away.

Anne Frankford's adultery has no malicious source whatsoever. She is seduced by Wendoll who has become obsessed with her beauty. Her recent marriage to Frankford is described by everyone as a perfect union, just as both she and her husband are described as perfect people. But this perfect couple have a fatal flaw in the form of Wendoll who worms his way between them. The unusual tactic that Heywood has chosen is not to have Frankford react with rage towards Anne at the discovery of the adultery. In fact he seems more shocked and embarrassed by it. This gives Anne very little to react to. Notice how she tries to coax Frankford into a violent reaction, but he says and does nothing. She anticipates the worst which never comes. Her greatest fear is that he will disfigure her with his sword and the speech gradually degenerates into begging pleas to do anything else except to scar her face. Heywood concentrates as much on the psychological effects of adultery as on its moral impact. You can convey Anne's grief and self-castigation by using the open 'o' vowel sounds ('Oh', 'No', 'once' 'souls', etc.) which evoke emotions. She uses them to focus Frankford's attention. The words have a great slow weight, so try not to rush through this speech. It requires your voice to be fully open.

[2] **abject** outcast

34

The Honest Whore (Part 1)
(1604) Thomas Dekker

Act 2, scene 1. Milan. A room in Bellafront's house.

Bellafront (20s) is a witty and successful courtesan. Count Hippolito, who is grieving for the death of Infeliche, his beloved, is brought to Bellafront's house to cheer him up. However, he proceeds to lecture her on the importance of constancy in love and castigates her for being a 'whore'. Despite this, Bellafront, attracted by his eloquence and sincere charm, falls in love with him, resolving to become 'honest'. But Hippolito remains immune to her advances and protestations and flees the scene in a violent rage, leaving his sword behind.

BELLAFRONT.
Stay yet a little longer. – No! quite gone!
Curs'd be that minute – for it was no more,
So soon a maid is chang'd into a whore –
Wherein I first fell; be it for ever black.
Yet why should sweet Hippolito shun mine eyes,
For whose true love I would become pure-honest,
Hate the world's mixtures,[1] and the smiles of gold?
Am I not fair? Why should he fly me then?
Fair creatures are desir'd, not scorned of men.
How many gallants have drunk healths to me,
Out of their dagger'd arms,[2] and thought them blest
Enjoying but mine eyes at prodigal feasts!
And does Hippolito detest my love?
Oh, sure their heedless lusts but flatt'red me;
I am not pleasing, beautiful, nor young.

[1] **mixtures** promiscuous intercourse
[2] **dagger'd arms** gallants often stabbed their arms letting the blood bleed into a glass of wine then drinking it to their mistress's health

Hippolito hath spied some ugly blemish,
Eclipsing all my beauties; I am foul.
'Harlot!' Ay, that's the spot that taints my soul.
What! has he left his weapon here behind him
And gone forgetful? O fit instrument
To let forth all the poison of my flesh!
Thy master hates me, 'cause my blood hath rang'd;[3]
But when 'tis forth, then he'll believe I'm changed.

As she is about to stab herself re-enter Hippolito.

[HIPPOLITO. Mad woman, what art doing?]

Either love me,
Or split my heart upon thy rapier's point;
Yet do not, neither; for thou then destroy'st
That which I love thee for, thy virtues. Here, here;

Gives sword to Hippolito.

Th'art crueller, and kill'st me with disdain;
To die so sheds no blood, yet 'tis worse pain.

Exit Hippolito.

Not speak to me! Not bid farewell? A scorn!
Hated! this must not be; some means I'll try.
Would all whores were as honest now as I!

Exits.

[*lines 523–545*]

COMMENTARY: Dekker's *The Honest Whore* is a two-part play
with an elaborate and exciting plot that includes three intrigues
that gradually knit together. It is also at different points a
comedy, a tragedy and a melodrama. In the main plot, the chaste
hero Hippolito mourns the death of his beloved Infeliche. He is
taken to the home of the courtesan Bellafront, whose advances he

---

[3] **blood hath rang'd** i.e. been sexually wayward
36

resists. She, however, falls madly in love with him and swears chastity as her new goal. When Hippolito learns that Infeliche is still alive he rushes away to marry her and Bellafront must content herself with marriage to another. The play is heavy on plot but contains some of the most lively dialogue and speeches in Jacobean drama. As this brief description suggests the full action of the play contains emotional twists and turns before all is righted in the end.

The actor playing Bellafront will have to decide how to reconcile the instantaneous transformations this character undergoes. Everything in this play is swiftly done, often without clear-cut motivation. But as she says, in a 'minute . . . a maid is chang'd into a whore.' Bellafront is almost continually operating at a high emotional pitch and is obsessed with herself and her predicament. Notice her repeated use of the pronouns 'I' and 'me'. The stakes are critical: life or death. Honour and morality do not concern her except as they relate to her fixation on Hippolito. When he brands her a 'harlot' she feels tainted and wounded. He is a most unusual man for her, a chaste man who resists her advances and her charms. This confuses her mightily. Notice how the speech is full of frantic exclamations. The character is racked from pillar to post. She is at her wits' end and ready to grab the nearest sword. The playwright plays games with her by having Hippolito enter and exit just as the scene reaches a climax, denying her the satisfaction of suicide and sending her reeling from the stage in a state of confusion.

Volpone
(1605) Ben Jonson

Act 3, scene 4. Venice. Volpone's bedroom.

Lady Would-be (40s–50s) is the wife of Sir Politic Would-be. Both are scatterbrained English tourists visiting Venice. In this scene Lady Would-be pays a visit to Volpone whom she has befriended although he despises her. She is shown into Volpone's bedroom by Nano, his servant.

LADY WOULD-BE.
I thank you, good sir. Pray you signify
Unto your patron I am here – This band[1]
Shows not my neck enough – I trouble you, sir;
Let me request you bid one of my women
Come hither to me. In good faith, I am dressed
Most favourably today! It is no matter;
'Tis well enough. (*Enter first serving woman.*) Look, see
  these petulant things!
How they have done this! . . .

       Come nearer. Is this curl
In his right place? or this? Why is this higher
Than all the rest? You ha' not washed your eyes yet?
Or do they not stand even i' your head?[2]
Where's your fellow? Call her . . .

Enter second serving woman.

        I pray you, view
This tire,[3] forsooth; are all things apt, or no?

---

[1] **band** neck ruff
[2] **You . . . head** i.e. can't you see straight
[3] **tire** coiffure
38

[FIRST WOMAN. One hair a little, here, sticks out,
    forsooth.]

Dost so, forsooth, and where was your dear sight
When it did so, forsooth? What now! Bird-eyed?[4]
And you too? Pray you both approach and mend it.
Now, by that light, I muse you're not ashamed!
I, that have preached these things so oft unto you,
Read you the principles, argued all the grounds,[5]
Disputed every fitness, every grace,
Called you to counsel of so frequent dressings –
Made you acquainted what an ample dowry
The knowledge of these things would be unto you,
Able, alone, to get you noble husbands
At your return;[6] and you, thus, to neglect it!
Besides, you seeing what a curious nation
Th'Italians are, what will they say of me?
'The English lady cannot dress herself.'
Here's a fine imputation to our country!
Well, go your ways, and stay i' the next room,
This fucus[7] was too coarse, too; it's no matter.
Good sir you'll give 'em good entertainment?

                                                [*lines 1–38*]

COMMENTARY: Jonson's *Volpone, or The Fox* is a classic comedy
that involves the duping of a group of legacy-hunters by a wily old
miser and his parasitical associate. Together Volpone and Mosca
invent schemes that yield a vast treasure of money, gold and
jewels. So creative are they that the plot of the play swells to fit
their imagination. In the end their greed gets the better of them,
they fall out and turn against one another, and are caught and

---

[4] **Bird-eyed** frightened stare
[5] **grounds** fundamentals (of hairdressing)
[6] **return** i.e. to England
[7] **fucus** face cosmetic

brought to justice. The sub-plot of the play concerns the adventures of an English knight, Sir Politic Would-be, and his grasping wife Lady Would-be. They are satirically drawn as English tourists abroad and are meant to be gross, comic caricatures.

Lady Would-be (an *arriviste* and would-be noblewoman) is loud in every sense of the word ('My madam with the everlasting voice. The bells in time of pestilence ne'er made like noise, or were in that perpetual motion.') She is in Venice with her equally foolish husband, so that she may study local fashions, hence her obsession with the minutiae of her appearance. The irony is, of course, that the harder she tries the more ridiculous she looks. Lady Would-be is a classic fashion-victim. Notice how she is endlessly fussing and fidgeting with her hair and accessories. She is vain, overdressed and overenunciates. She babbles on and uses more words than necessary to say anything. See how she flies into a fit when she thinks one of her curls is out of place. The character must have an audience for every word and gesture. She is a random performer who plays to the whole house. She wants to present a perfect appearance to Volpone and this is a preamble to a scene of comic flirtation. Her reactions to everything, particularly her appearance, have been inspired by books of etiquette.

The Winter's Tale
(1611) William Shakespeare

Act 3, scene 2. Sicilia. A place of justice.

Hermione (20s) is the virtuous wife and queen of Leontes, King of Sicilia. Her husband has falsely convinced himself that she has been unfaithful to him with his friend Polixenes. The king's jealousy gets out of hand and Hermione is forced into a trial where she is indicted and condemned for adultery and treason. Here she defends herself in an open court.

HERMIONE.
  Since what I am to say must be but that
  Which contradicts my accusation, and
  The testimony on my part no other
  But what comes from myself, it shall scarce boot[1] me
  To say 'not guilty'. Mine integrity,
  Being counted falsehood, shall, as I express[2] it,
  Be so received. But thus: if powers divine
  Behold our human actions, as they do,
  I doubt not then but innocence shall make
  False accusation blush and tyranny
  Tremble at patience. You, my lord, best know,
  Who least will seem to do so, my past life
  Hath been as continent,[3] as chaste, as true,
  As I am now unhappy; which is more
  Than history can pattern,[4] though devised
  And played to take[5] spectators. For behold me –

[1] **boot** help
[2] **express** reveal
[3] **continent** self-restrained
[4] **pattern** match
[5] **take** captivate

A fellow[6] of the royal bed, which owe[7]
A moiety[8] of the throne, a great king's daughter,
The mother to a hopeful prince – here standing
To prate and talk for life and honour 'fore
Who please[9] to come and hear. For life, I prize it
As I weigh[10] grief, which I would spare.[11] For honour,
'Tis a derivative from me to mine,[12]
And only that I stand for.[13] I appeal
To your own conscience,[14] sir, before Polixenes
Came to your court, how I was in your grace,
How merited to be so; since he came,
With what encounter so uncurrent I
Have strained t'appear thus;[15] if one jot beyond
The bound of honour, or in act or will
That way inclining, hardened be the hearts
Of all that hear me, and my near'st of kin
Cry fie upon my grave!

[*lines 22–53*]

COMMENTARY: Shakespeare's *The Winter's Tale* is a play that begins in tragic circumstances but ends in retribution and fantastic renewal. King Leontes of Sicilia unreasonably suspects his wife Hermione of being unfaithful with Polixenes, Leontes' boyhood friend. He further believes that the child Hermione is carrying is Polixenes' as well, even though Leontes is the true father. Leontes throws Hermione into prison where she gives

[6] **fellow** sharer
[7] **which owe** who owns
[8] **moiety** portion, half
[9] **Who please** whosoever pleases
[10] **weigh** value
[11] **spare** avoid, do without
[12] **'Tis. . . mine** i.e. it will descend from me to my children
[13] **stand for** stand up for, defend
[14] **conscience** judgement
[15] **With . . . thus** i.e. I ask what unacceptable behaviour has brought me here, disgraced and on trial

birth to a daughter Perdita. He disowns the baby and has it cast out into the wilderness. Their son Mamillius is also taken from Hermione and later dies. Leontes' rage continues and he brings Hermione to trial as a traitor and adulteress. At the trial, on learning of her son's death, she swoons and is taken into care by Paulina, who hatches a plan to spirit her away to safety and tells Leontes that she has died. The news of this finally makes Leontes see his grievous error. After an interval of sixteen years, and a romantic sub-plot that consumes Acts Four and Five, Hermione, in the guise of a statue, is 'brought back to life' by Leontes' genuine remorse. It is one of the most moving theatrical scenes in Shakespeare. The play ends happily as the couple are reunited with their missing daughter Perdita.

Hermione is one of Shakespeare's most virtuous characters. She is open and generous in her affections towards everyone which is why Leontes mistakes her friendship with Polixenes for adultery. In the trial scene the actor must remember that the character has just recently given birth while imprisoned. You must act against her physical state of weakness as you defend yourself wholeheartedly against the charge of adultery. Your innocence must be above reproach. Notice how dignified Hermione is when she speaks. She thinks mainly of her children and the husband who accuses her. The word 'integrity' is crucial for her. Despite all of the emotional pressures she is under, Hermione's speech is a masterful defence of honour and right. These are the kinds of concepts that the character repeatedly calls on to aid her cause. She never resorts to sentiment or marital manipulation. Note that the verse is very balanced and the sentences complex and involved. You must keep voice and breath strong throughout and never break down into tears. Hermione continually fights them back so that her appeal to the king's conscience will be heard. The legal phrasings must be paired with the genuine grace that this character possesses. She knows her place, her virtue and her rights as a wife, mother and queen.

The White Devil
(1612) John Webster

Act 4, scene 2. Rome. The House of Convertites.

Vittoria Corombona (20s) has been denounced as an adulteress and a murderess and been confined in a house of convertites (reformed prostitutes). In league with her lover the Duke of Brachiano, she willingly assented to the death of her husband Camillo. She is visited here by Brachiano and her brother Flamineo. Vittoria and Brachiano are in a heated argument. He has accused her of receiving love letters.

VITTORIA.
  What have I gain'd by thee but infamy?
  Thou hast stain'd the spotless honour of my house,
  And frighted thence noble society:
  Like those, which sick o' th' palsy, and retain
  Ill-scenting foxes[1] 'bout them, are still shunn'd
  By those of choicer nostrils.
  What do you call this house?
  Is this your palace? Did not the judge style it
  A house of penitent whores? Who sent me to it?
  Who hath the honour to advance Vittoria
  To this incontinent[2] college? Is't not you?
  Is't not your high preferment?[3] Go, go brag
  How many ladies you have undone, like me.
  Fare you well sir; let me hear no more of you.
  I had a limb corrupted to an ulcer,
    But I have cut it off: and now I'll go

---

[1] **ill-scenting foxes** i.e. the strong scent of the fox was thought to cure palsy
[2] **incontinent** lacking in self-restraint in sexual appetite
[3] **preferment** advancement in status or position

Weeping to heaven on crutches. For your gifts,
I will return them all; and I do wish
That I could make you full executor
To all my sins. O that I could toss myself
Into a grave as quickly: for all thou art worth
I'll not shed one tear more; – I'll burst first.

She throws herself on a bed.

[*lines 107–127*]

COMMENTARY: Webster's *The White Devil* is a tale of jealousy
and death in which the beautiful Vittoria Corombona encourages
the affections of the Duke of Brachiano eventually leading to the
murder of her husband Camillo. The love affair and murder are
partly engineered by her diabolical brother Flamineo, who also
plots the death of Brachiano's wife Isabella. A whirlwind of
passion and revenge follow from these incidents as all three
characters die ignominiously in the end.

As the tension of the previous three scenes has mounted and
reached a fevered pitch, the once cool and collected Vittoria
begins to crack. Brachiano suspects her of receiving love letters
(which have actually been written by her brother Flamineo) and
these ignite a violent argument between the lovers. Vittoria's
resentment spews forth in this speech; she has lost fame and
honour as well as the world from which she came and she feels
like an infected thing. These thoughts are what she hurls at
Brachiano in her defence. Webster's writing is simple and direct;
although the speech is in blank verse many of the lines have a
break midway so are spoken as short units and this gives the
speech a marvellous simplicity. There is also room for pauses and
reproachful silences. The images she uses are vile but arresting.
Notice that the speech is littered with questions which are used to
beat down Brachiano. As the passion of speech swells, Vittoria
uses more and more rich vowels to express her emotion culminat-
ing in the extraordinary phrase 'I'll burst first.' The actor should
realise that the simple construction of the lines leaves lots of room
for performance. You are not limited by heavy rhetoric or
complex metaphors. This is one of those Jacobean speeches that

sounds wholly natural and spontaneous when you speak lines like 'Go, go brag how many ladies you have undone, like me.' You come away with the feeling that there is nothing artificial about Vittoria. She has a real flesh-and-blood presence.

The Maid's Tragedy
(1612–13) Francis Beaumont & John Fletcher

Act 5, scene 1. Rhodes. The King's bedchamber.

Evadne (20s) has been married off by royal command to Amintor, a noble courtier. Neither of them is in love with the other. In fact, Evadne is the King's secret mistress and Amintor had been betrothed to his true love Aspatia. The King has engineered the marriage to mask his on-going affair with Evadne. However, Melantius, Evadne's brother, learns of this deception and seeks vengeance for both his wronged friend Amintor and his sister. He persuades her to murder the King in the very bed in which he dishonoured her. In this soliloquy she is preparing herself to do that deed.

EVADNE.
    The night grows horrible; and all about me
    Like my black purpose. Oh, the conscience
    Of a lost virgin! whither wilt thou pull me?
    To what things, dismal as the depth of hell,
    Wilt thou provoke me? Let no woman dare
    From this hour be disloyal, if her heart be flesh,
    If she have blood, and can fear. 'Tis a daring
    Above that desperate fool's that left his peace,
    And went to sea to fight. 'Tis so many sins,
    An age cannot repent 'em; and so great,
    The gods want mercy for! Yet I must through 'em.
    I have begun a slaughter on my honour,
    And I must end it there.

She opens the curtains of the inner stage discovering the King in bed.

    – He sleeps. Good Heavens!

47

Why give you peace to this untemperate[1] beast,
That hath so long transgress'd you? I must kill him,
And I will do't bravely: The mere joy
Tells me I merit in it. Yet I must not
Thus tamely do it, as he sleeps – that were
To rock[2] him to another world: My vengeance
Shall take him waking, and then lay before him
The number of his wrongs and punishments.
I'll shape[3] his sins like Furies, till I waken
His evil angel, his sick conscience;
And then I'll strike him dead.

[*lines 24–38*]

COMMENTARY: Beaumont and Fletcher's *The Maid's Tragedy* weaves two romantic plots together to create one disastrous outcome. The play focuses on the frustrated love of Amintor and Aspatia. After the King dissolves their engagement he forces Amintor to wed Evadne, the royal mistress. The results of this mis-match are tragic for all four characters. The wronged Aspatia kills herself by falling on Amintor's sword and Evadne in a fit of guilty conscience goes into the King's bedroom and kills him by stabbing him to death, after which both she and Amintor commit suicide. The play distributes its tragic impact among all four characters without singling out any one as the central hero or heroine.

Evadne's speech is meant to remind us of Hamlet's soliloquy when he finds Claudius praying and debates with himself whether to kill him or not. Like Hamlet, Evadne's chief fear is that she will send the King's soul not to hell but to heaven ('to rock him to another world'). She wants him to suffer and in the scene right after this speech the King awakens and struggles with her and dies in the end. This speech starts a prolonged death scene. The darkness and apprehension built into this speech must be echoed in the words which are full of brooding vowel sounds. Notice how

---

[1] **untemperate** i.e. excessively indulgent, especially in sexual passion
[2] **To rock** i.e. gently send
[3] **shape** (sometimes appears as 'shake')

the words plunge downwards ('dismal as the depth of hell'). There is a ghoulish 'black' atmosphere and also the notion of a woman who has been wronged and systematically made to suffer from the loss of her virginity. So the lines are full of stress and conflict. The iambic pentameter lines frequently have a mid-line caesura or pause, which gives the character time to think and convince herself of the best way to proceed in the murder. As she observes the sleeping King her courage is fuelled by hatred. She wants him to awaken so that she can confront him with his sins like the mythical Furies of Greek tragedy and ensure that his soul is damned for eternity. To do otherwise would be too tame. Thus she will satisfy her thirst for revenge and repay the suffering she has experienced. This is the same bed where she lost her virginity to the King so the motivation to commit the act has a deep visual symbolism for her as she revisits the scene of her own undoing.

The Duchess of Malfi
(1612–14) John Webster

Act 1, scene 2. Naples. A room in a palace.

The Duchess of Malfi (20s) is a young widow. She lives at court under the watchful and suspicious eyes of her twin brother Ferdinand, Duke of Calabria and another brother the Cardinal. Both brothers, motivated by family pride and avarice, want to prevent the Duchess from remarrying. They install the unscrupulous Bosola in her household as their spy. She, however, has fallen in love with Antonio, her steward, and decides, against her brothers' wishes, to propose to him herself. She does so in this scene by symbolically placing her wedding ring on his finger. In this speech she explains her direct approach.

DUCHESS.
    The misery of us, that are born great,
    We are forc'd to woo, because none dare woo us:
    And as a tyrant doubles[1] with his words,
    And fearfully equivocates:[2] so we
    Are forc'd to express our violent passions
    In riddles, and in dreams, and leave the path
    Of simple virtue, which was never made
    To seem the thing it is not. Go, go brag
    You have left me heartless, mine is in your bosom,
    I hope 'twill multiply love there. You do tremble:
    Make not your heart so dead a piece of flesh
    To fear, more than to love me. Sir, be confident,
    What is't distracts[3] you? This is flesh, and blood, sir,
    'Tis not the figure cut in alabaster

---

[1] **doubles** i.e. acts deceitfully or evasively
[2] **equivocates** i.e. uses ambiguity to hide the truth
[3] **distracts** confuses

50

Kneels at my husband's tomb. Awake, awake, man,
I do here put off all vain ceremony,
And only do appear to you, a young widow
That claims you for her husband, and like a widow,
I use but half a blush[4] in't.

[*lines 360–378*]

COMMENTARY: Webster's *The Duchess of Malfi* is considered to be one of the most moving tragedies in English drama. The plot concerns the disastrous consequences that follow from the liaison between the virtuous and widowed Duchess and her steward Antonio. The protectiveness and jealousy of her two brothers – based on dynastic and economic stratagems – eventually lead to her violent and diabolical death by strangulation. The play is celebrated because it manages to mix the grosser excesses of Jacobean revenge tragedy with heightened poetic passages that describe the Duchess's plight and state of mind in moving detail. Her death scene is one of the most memorable and pathetic moments in drama.

This is a rare scene in which a woman woos a man. Throughout the play the Duchess is forced to descend from her high position of nobility. First she falls in love and then secretly marries a man who is basically her servant. Here she begins the process. The actor at this moment must cast aside all pretensions to grandeur and speak simply and directly to the man she loves. She sees her greatness as a heavy burden which love lightens. Notice the tension in the speech between passion and control. Although the speech is quite real and anchored to the earth the Duchess is a poetic creature who takes flight and will reach into another world for images. Throughout the play she is besieged by 'riddles' and 'dreams'. In this speech notice how she speaks in riddles and paradoxes, wooing Antonio indirectly. It is quite clear too that Antonio is both nervous and out of his depth, so part of the speech is aimed at reassuring him. The actor must compensate for the fact that the character's proposal is very abrupt; we are given no hint of her intention early on. As she speaks the speech she has

---

[4] **half a blush** i.e. not a virgin

51

her maid hidden behind a screen, witnessing the whole proposal scene, so the monologue is delivered in an atmosphere of tension, suspicion and uncertainty. Truth and honesty are at a premium in this play and the Duchess, as she shows here, is one of the few characters who give themselves licence to speak spontaneously. The speech has an easy flow from word to word and image to image. The delivery should be natural and avoid any artificial versification. Use the blank verse as though it were everyday speech.

The Changeling

(*c.* 1622) Thomas Middleton & William Rowley

Act 4, scene 1. Spain. Alsemero's apartment in the castle of Alicante.

Beatrice-Joanna, the wilful daughter of the Governor of Alicante, has just married the Valencian gentleman Alsemero. The marriage is a wish fulfilled. But earlier in the play she rid herself of her unwanted fiancé Alonso, murdered by her dutiful servant De Flores. In exchange for the murder, De Flores deflowers Beatrice in the scene immediately preceding the opening of this one. Here Beatrice expresses her fears that she has deceived her new husband and that her deceit will be discovered if she proves to be pregnant. In her husband's apartment she finds a strange closet full of potions and a book of tests to expose signs of pregnancy.

BEATRICE.
    This fellow has undone[1] me endlessly;
    Never was bride so fearfully distress'd.
    The more I think upon th' ensuing night,
    And whom I am to cope with[2] in embraces:
    One both ennobled in blood and mind,
    So clear in understanding – that's my plague now, –
    Before whose judgement will my fault appear
    Like malefactors' crimes before tribunals.
    There is no hiding on't, the more I dive
    Into my own distress. How a wise man
    Stands for[3] a great calamity! There's no venturing
    Into his bed, what course soe'er I light upon,
    Without my shame, which may grow up to danger.

[1] **undone** ruined
[2] **cope with** encounter, contend with
[3] **Stands for** stands open to

He cannot but in justice strangle me
As I lie by him – as a cheater use me;
'Tis a precious craft to play with a false die
Before a cunning gamester. Here's his closet;
The key left in't, and he abroad i' th' park!
Sure't was forgot; I'll be so bold as look in't.

Opens closet.

Bless me! a right physician's closet 'tis,
Set round with vials; every one her mark too.
Sure he does practise physic for his own use,
Which may be safely call'd your great man's wisdom.[4]
What manuscript lies here? 'The Book of Experiment,
Call'd Secrets in Nature.' So 'tis; 'tis so.
(*Reads.*) 'How to know whether a woman be with child
    or no.'
I hope I am not yet, – if he should try though!
Let me see (*Reads.*) 'folio forty-five,' here 'tis,
The leaf tuck'd down upon't, the place suspicious.
(*Reads.*) 'If you would know whether a woman be with
    child or not, give her two spoonfuls of the white
    water in glass C –'
Where's that glass C? Oh, yonder, I see't now –
(*Reads.*) 'and if she be with child, she sleeps full twelve
    hours after; if not, not.'
None of that water comes into my belly;
I'll know you from a hundred; I could break you now,
Or turn you into milk and so beguile
The master of the mystery; but I'll look to you.
Ha! that which is next is ten times worse:
(*Reads.*) 'How to know whether a woman be a maid[5] or
    not;'
If that should be appli'd, what would become of me?

4 **Which . . . wisdom** i.e. since it will protect him from poisoning
5 **maid** i.e. a virgin

54

Belike he has a strong faith of my purity,
That never yet made proof; but this he calls
(*Reads*.) 'A merry sleight,[6] but true experiment; the
    author Antonius Mizaldus. Give the party you
    suspect the quantity of a spoonful of the water in
    the glass M, which, upon her that is a maid, makes
    three several effects: 'twill make her incontinently[7]
    gape, then fall into a sudden sneezing, last into a
    violent laughing; else, dull, heavy, and lumpish.'
Where had I been?
I fear it; yet 'tis seven hours to bedtime.

[*lines 1–56*]

COMMENTARY: *The Changeling* is one of the most powerful and unremitting of the Jacobean revenge tragedies. At its centre is a psychological study of a capricious young woman who gradually 'changes' from an innocent to a victimiser to a victim as the result of a sudden crime of passion. The relationship between Beatrice and the grotesque De Flores is the story of beauty and the beast. De Flores worships her from afar and then takes control over her when he murders on her behalf. The tragedy continually progresses from bad to worse as the two oddly matched 'lovers' die in a double death. Madness and sexual passion propel the action.

In this frantic speech Beatrice is consumed with thoughts of two men at once: De Flores and Alsemero. Her thoughts 'change' from one to the other in an ever-shifting state of mounting neurosis. Her great secret is that she has surrendered to De Flores sexually and now faces her wedding night with Alsemero. The closet in the room contains two types of tests: one for virginity and the other for pregnancy. The discovery of these weird concoctions and the tests they perform sets off her worst fears and anxieties. Notice how Beatrice is both full of wonder and loathing as she reads the manuscript. The actor must translate these two mismatched emotions to the audience. But that double effect

[6] **sleight** cunning trick
[7] **incontinently** immediately

underscores Beatrice's capacity as a character: she has boldly blundered forwards and then watches herself as she falls from grace. The speech is also full of acute forebodings of justice and retribution. Every step of the way throughout the play Beatrice knows she will have to pay the price for her shame.

Women Beware Women

(*c.* 1623) Thomas Middleton

Act 1, scene 2. Florence. A room in Livia's palatial residence.

Isabella (16–18) is the daughter of Fabritio, and Livia's niece. Her father has arranged a marriage for her with Gaurdiano's foolish ward. Livia has argued it is unfair that her niece must marry a man whom she neither likes nor loves. In this scene Isabella has just seen her future husband and here she expresses her opinion of him in a long aside.

ISABELLA.

                       Marry a fool!
Can there be greater misery to a woman
That means to keep her days true to her husband,
And know no other man, so virtue wills it!
Why, how can I obey and honour him,
But I must needs commit idolatry?[1]
A fool is but the image of a man,
And that but ill made neither.[2] Oh the heartbreakings
Of miserable maids, where love's enforced!
The best condition is but bad enough:
When women have their choices, commonly
They do but buy their thraldoms, and bring great
        portions[3]
To men to keep 'em in subjection:
As if a fearful prisoner should bribe
The keeper to be good to him, yet lies in[4] still.
And glad of a good usage, a good look sometimes.

[1] **idolatry** (used here to mean the worship of senseless objects)
[2] **neither** i.e. for all that, too
[3] **portions** dowries
[4] **lies in** remains in prison

57

By'r Lady, no misery surmounts a woman's.
Men buy their slaves, but women buy their masters.
Yet honesty and love makes all this happy
And, next to angels', the most blest estate.[5]
That Providence, that has made ev'ry poison
Good for some use, and sets four warring elements[6]
At peace in man, can make a harmony
In things that are most strange to human reason.
Oh, but this marriage!

[lines 164–188]

COMMENTARY: Middleton's *Women Beware Women* has a plot full of intrigue and revenge with themes that focus on the corruption of women. As a result it has a rich array of female roles in which various characters show different aspects of womanhood under assault. There are fewer plays in English drama which dissect male/female relationships with more passion and power. The tragedy lies in the degeneration of innocence which results from the unending drives towards power and the satisfaction of sexual appetites.

Isabella's situation, being made to marry an inappropriate mate, is typical of the cruel reversals of fortune that characters are forced to suffer in this play. Mercantile and economic factors play a large role in the proceedings. Notice how the notions of 'buying' and 'slavery' feature in the speech. In Isabella's case she is being made to marry a complete fool and is being treated as a trading commodity in the marriage negotiations. Standing on-stage, too, is her uncle Hippolito who has incestuous designs on her. The speech catches Isabella between two undesirable poles; folly and incest. The speech itself is an expiation of all the confusion that women are made to suffer when trapped in such a man-made situation. It is a catalogue of female frustration and anger delivered openly as if to vent all the feelings that have been building under pressure. The tension is increased by the fact that

[5] estate condition
[6] four . . . elements the four natural elements – earth, air, fire and water – were thought to correspond to the same elements in man

the actor must voice these sentiments openly. In her eyes marriage is a farce but this arranged marriage to a fool is a literal farce. The order and balance of the universe are thrown into disorder and imbalance by this kind of act. Isabella is a bright character who sees her fate – and the fate of women – all too clearly. The speech must have an almost didactic commitment. She has discovered an essential piece of wisdom and wants to share it with the audience. Notice how the speech ascends higher and higher only to drop back to earth in the final line.

'Tis Pity She's a Whore
(1625–33) John Ford

Act 5, scene 1. Parma. A balcony.

Annabella (16–18) is the beautiful daughter of Florio and sister to the brilliant Giovanni. She has several suitors. However, her brother has become infatuated with her, and she too has found herself attracted to him. They become incestuous lovers. When Annabella realises that she has become pregnant she decides to marry one of her suitors, Soranzo, to save her honour. After the marriage he discovers her state and demands to know who her lover is; she refuses to reveal him and plans to take her own life.

ANNABELLA.
Pleasures, farewell, and all ye thriftless minutes
Wherein false joys have spun a weary life.
To these my fortunes now I take my leave.
Thou, precious Time, that swiftly rid'st in post[1]
Over the world, to finish up the race
Of my last fate, here stay thy restless course,
And bear to ages that are yet unborn
A wretched, woeful woman's tragedy.
My conscience now stands up[2] against my lust
With depositions charactered[3] in guilt,
And tells me I am lost: now I confess
Beauty that clothes the outside of the face
Is cursed if it be not clothed with grace.
Here like a turtle[4] (mewed up[5] in a cage)

[1] **swiftly . . . post** rides posthorses quickly
[2] **stands up** bears witness
[3] **charactered** inscribed
[4] **turtle** turtledove
[5] **mewed up** imprisoned

Unmated, I converse with air and walls,
And descant[6] on my vile unhappiness.
O Giovanni, that hast had the spoil
Of thine own virtues and my modest fame,[7]
Would thou hadst been less subject to those stars
That luckless reigned at my nativity:
O would the scourge due to my black offence
Might pass from thee, that I alone might feel
The torment of an uncontrolled flame.

[lines 1–23]

COMMENTARY: Ford's 'Tis Pity She's a Whore follows the
fortunes of two star-crossed lovers who happen to be brother and
sister. It is a kind of profane Romeo and Juliet in which incest
replaces chasteness. The incestuous coupling happens quite early
in the first act and the rest of the play becomes a delayed reaction
to this disastrous mating. Both lovers die in the end but not
before the entire society depicted in the play is shattered. In the
final scene Giovanni enters with Annabella's heart on the end of
his dagger.

The unfortunate Annabella carries the brand of 'whore'
although her suffering at this point is largely inflicted by her
conscience. A stiff morality hangs over the play causing much of
the inner tension that creates conflict for the characters.
Annabella has travelled a long distance from the Juliet of
Shakespeare's play and her balcony scenes are really like death
scenes; she knows the end is inevitable. Night cloaks the crime
and the stars rule it. The actor should also remember that by this
point in the play Annabella is alone and almost a prisoner in her
own house which is why she sounds so totally isolated in the
speech. Incest has made her a hostage to fortune. Throughout the
speech a Friar stands unseen below listening to her so the speech
becomes a kind of confession. Annabella's guilt is certainly
seeking exoneration from its torment. Notice that the speech
takes place at night and is full of a darkness that is enhanced by

[6] **descant** sing
[7] **fame** reputation

the atmosphere. Also note that the lines get more and more extended and harder to control as the soliloquy turns into a lament. Annabella, as is shown throughout the play, is not a fierce rebel like her brother Giovanni and the full impact of the incest seems to weigh on her alone. As the play proceeds, the greater the pressure she bears the less capable she becomes of acting.

Life is a Dream
(1635) Calderón [Pedro Calderón de la Barca]

Act 1. Inside a mountainous tower somewhere in Poland.

Rosaura (18–20) has found her way into a barren mountainous terrain where she discovers the unfortunate Prince Segismundo chained in a tower like an animal. She left Moscow, 'in search of honour's satisfaction', to follow her enemy Astolfo, Duke of Moscow, to the Polish court. Disguised as a man and accompanied by her servant Clarion she has lost her way. She hears Segismundo's melancholic outbursts and stays to listen as he tells the story of his misery. Then she answers him.

ROSAURA.
    I see you with astonishment.
    I listen to your history
    With such complete amazement, I
    Neither know what I should say to you
    Or ask; unless it be that heaven,
    Perhaps, has sent me here, so I
    Should not feel pity for my own
    Misfortune, but seek the consolation
    Of another's misery and see
    If what they say is true: that seeing
    Someone else's grief must always
    Offer one relief. They say there was
    A wise man once who, being poor,
    Had no food, and found his sustenance
    In herbs and berries. 'You won't find
    Any person worse than me,' he'd say.
    But when he turned and looked behind
    He saw another man who, as

He went along, stayed close to him,
And bent to eat the leaves he'd thrown
Away. So I, complaining of
My own misfortune, was on the point
Of saying to myself: 'Oh, who
In this entire world can be
Less fortunate than I?', when your
Wretched fate became the answer
To my question, your misery
The measure of my joy; for you,
I know, would eagerly accept
My suffering as your pleasure.
If my misfortunes were to make
You happier, I'd gladly give
You some of them. Perhaps you'd like
To hear my story.

Translated by Gwynne Edwards

COMMENTARY: Calderón's *Life is a Dream* starts as a tragedy and ends as an uplifting lesson about man's capacity to exercise his own free will. Segismundo, heir to the throne of Poland, begins the action chained in a tower like a beast. At his birth a prophecy decreed that he would be a tyrant if allowed to become king. As a result his father King Basilio had him immediately imprisoned in the tower. However, King Basilio plans to abdicate his throne in favour of his nephew Astolfo, Duke of Moscow. Before committing himself he decides to test Segismundo by putting him on the throne for a trial period of rule. Drugged and sleeping, he is taken from his prison and awakens to all the splendour of a baroque palace. With the ferocity of a caged animal suddenly set free, he lashes out and tyrannises everyone around him, seeming to prove the prophecy. Drugged once again, he is returned to his tower and awakens to ponder what it has all meant. Soon afterwards Segismundo is liberated from his tower again and, having learned his lesson well, harnesses his temper and rules like a model prince.

Rosaura is a leading figure in the sub-plot of the play that focuses on honour wronged and honour restored. On her arduous journey from Moscow to Poland, in pursuit of Astolfo who has wronged her, she comes upon the imprisoned Segismundo here at the very start of the play. We know little about her except that she is dressed as a man, seems to be in flight but stops to show enormous pity and feeling for a fellow human being. She uses his grief in order to stimulate her own, finding that there are people less fortunate in the world than she. For the most part, her speech is written in a pattern of eight-syllable lines. The verse is expected to grow and swell as the character speaks. Note how she stresses the 's' sound in words like 'astonishment', 'history', 'amazement', and a similar sound in every line of the speech ending in the word 'story'. Her function in the play is to be a kind of ministering angel and later on she becomes an avenging angel against Astolfo, though in the end the two are harmoniously united. Like every character in the play she has two sides, one humane and one violent. Here the former is on display and the actor should not be too timid to show a full-blown empathy in this speech.

The Misanthrope
(1666) Molière [Jean Baptiste Poquelin]

Act 3, scene 5. Paris. A salon in Célimène's house.

Célimène (18–20), a Parisian socialite and beloved of Alceste, the 'Misanthrope', is engaged in a conversation with a friend and rival Arsinoé. Arsinoé tries to upset Célimène by describing the 'ugly gossip and obscene surmises' that have been spread about her. Célimène answers her in this monologue.

CELIMENE.
    Madam, I haven't taken you amiss;
    I'm very much obliged to you for this;
    And I'll at once discharge the obligation
    By telling you about *your* reputation.
    You've been so friendly as to let me know
    What certain people say of me, and so
    I mean to follow your benign example
    By offering you a somewhat similar sample.
    The other day, I went to an affair
    And found some most distinguished people there
    Discussing piety, both false and true.
    The conversation soon came round to you.
    Alas! Your prudery and bustling zeal
    Appeared to have a very slight appeal.
    Your affectation of a grave demeanour,
    Your endless talk of virtue and of honour,
    The aptitude of your suspicious mind
    For finding sin where there is none to find,
    Your towering self-esteem, that pitying face
    With which you contemplate the human race,
    Your sermonisings and your sharp aspersions

On people's pure and innocent diversions –
All these were mentioned, Madam, and, in fact,
Were roundly and concertedly attacked.
'What good,' they said, 'are all those outward shows,
When everything belies her pious pose?
She prays incessantly; but then, they say,
She beats her maids and cheats them of their pay;
She shows her zeal in every holy place,
But still she's vain enough to paint her face;
She holds that naked statues are immoral,
But with a naked *man* she'd have no quarrel.'
Of course, I said to everybody there
That they were being viciously unfair;
But still they were disposed to criticise you,
And all agreed that someone should advise you
To leave the morals of the world alone,
And worry rather more about your own.
They felt that one's self-knowledge should be great
Before one thinks of setting others straight;
That one should learn the art of living well
Before one threatens other men with hell,
And that the Church is best equipped, no doubt,
To guide our souls and root our vices out.
Madam, you're too intelligent, I'm sure,
To think my motives anything but pure
In offering you this counsel – which I do
Out of a zealous interest in you.

Translated by Richard Wilbur

COMMENTARY: Molière's *The Misanthrope* is one of the great studies of comic character in classical drama. Alceste is self-righteously opposed to the superficiality of the society in which he lives and to some degree he is right. The world in which he moves is full of gossip, slander, lawsuits and false love and Alceste is himself being sued in the courts for libel, which only compounds

67

his misanthropy. He is in love with the independent Célimène whose flirtatiousness with other men and tolerance of society's foibles only adds to his despair. She is his comic flaw and their incompatibility leads to his departure from Paris at the end of the play on a very sour note.

The speech is written entirely in rhyming couplets, as is the whole play. They are not to be spoken preciously or too poetically. Use the rhymes as a sarcastic weapon. As you go through the speech always work to the end of a thought which usually stops with punctuation, yet avoid falling into a sing-song pattern that will only make the speech sound artificial and unconvincing. The rhyming should sound spontaneous, exactly as if the character is minting the thoughts as she speaks. Célimène speaks with poisoned politeness: her devastating wit masks any outward show of anger. It is important to keep the latter under control at all times. Remember that Arsinoé has accused Célimène of being a notorious coquette. This is a serious charge and you must decide how Célimène's words can be used for vengeance. What you do is use language to expose and defame the other party. In this society the strict rhythm of speech locks the character into place, but the information released can be your weapon. Never lose sight of Célimène's flirtatious and zestful personality. She is the gayest and most carefree character in the play and the very opposite of a hypocritical prude like Arsinoé.

Phedra
(1677) Jean Racine

Act 2. Troezen (a city near Athens). Somewhere inside the palace.

Phedra (30s), the wife of Theseus, King of Athens, has confessed to her nurse that she is dying of love for her stepson Hippolytus. The passion was instigated by the goddess Venus' curse. Stabbing pangs of morality and conscience weigh heavily on Phedra and lead her to make a series of agonising speeches. She finally declares her love to Hippolytus; he tries not to hear what she is saying, so she pursues him further in this speech.

PHEDRA.
Ah! You understood me all too well.
I have revealed too much for 'misinterpretation';
Now recognise a woman torn apart by passion.
I am in love. Guiltless in my own eyes, my love
For you is not a thing of which I can approve.
It was not cowardice or compliance bred the poison
Of the insane desire that now destroys my reason.
Venus has sought me out for her revengeful curse;
You may abhor me, but I loathe myself far worse.
I call the Gods to witness, those cruel Gods, that flood
My loins with fire, like all those of our cursèd blood;
Gods who seduce weak human beings, as they please,
From the straight paths of love to perverse heresies.
I tried to fly from you, but it was useless. Malice
And desperation made me drive you from the palace.
I sought your hatred; it alone could strengthen me.
What was the upshot of my futile strategy?
You loathed me all the more, I did not love you less:
Your grace and beauty only grew in your distress.

I pined in tears, shrivelled in fire, past remedy;
You could have seen, if you had ever looked at me.
What have I said? Can you imagine I enjoyed
Confessing shame I tried expressly to avoid?
Take your revenge on me and on my love together.
Show yourself the son of your heroic father,
And slay another monster, the most dangerous,
Theseus' wife that dared to love Hippolytus!
Only this monster sees its death as a reward;
Here is my heart; here is where you must sheathe your
    sword.
Kill me. Or, if I'm thought too vile an enemy,
Should your hate begrudge me so sweet an agony,
Or if your hand would be defiled by such foul blood,
Then do not plunge it in yourself – give me the sword.
Give it to me.

[lines 640–673]
Translated by Robert David MacDonald

COMMENTARY: Racine's *Phedra* is one of the most unrelenting of the great classical tragedies. All of the characters are victims of Fate and the hatred of the gods. Phedra, wife of Theseus, herself the daughter of Minos and a descendant of the Sun, is passionately in love with her stepson Hippolytus. Her feelings of guilt are overwhelming. Hippolytus is in love with Aricia and is shocked when he learns of Phedra's passion for him. The sudden return of Theseus, who was believed dead, sends the tragedy spiralling to its disastrous conclusion. Through their monologues and dialogues all of the characters express a torment that is unbearable. Death is almost a welcome relief from the tension.

Phedra's confession pours out of her as a torturous rant. She is like a woman possessèd. This kind of tragic behaviour is very difficult to play without lapsing into melodramatic posturing, so you must think of each line as a fresh wound you are suffering. Try and internalise everything that is happening to Phedra. All the torment she is suffering is against her will and reason. The actor continually has to struggle against Phedra's deep emotions.

This is not an intellectual dilemma, but a highly charged and deeply felt turmoil brought on by passion. Practically all of the lines are end-stopped, meaning that the energy of the speech is contained in each of the separate lines of verse. English cannot duplicate or adequately translate the sound and poetic power of the twelve-syllable French alexandrine with its climactic break in each line. You must try to remember that each sentence is a separate unit of energy that, like a series of waves, gets stronger and stronger as the tide of passion breaks against the shore. The effect should be of unrelenting power that builds and builds. Pick out one or two words in each sentence that can withstand the burden of emotion. They are there for you to use like the rungs of a ladder as you descend into the abyss of passion. Notice that one of Phedra's last words is 'plunge'; that is exactly the direction you have to follow with this speech.

The Game of Love and Chance
(1730) Pierre Marivaux

Act 1, scene 1. Paris. A salon in a town house.

Silvia (18–20s), the daughter of Monsieur Orgon, a rich merchant, is set to marry Dorante, the son of a family friend, who she has never met. In this speech she speaks to her maid Lisette about what there is to look for in a husband beyond charm and good looks.

SILVIA.
You don't know what you're talking about. In marriage it's more often a question of dealing with a man of reason than a man of charm. In short, all I want in a husband is a good temper, and that is much more difficult to find than you would believe. They all sing his praises, but which of them has actually lived with him? Men often will give a false impression in public of themselves, especially if they've any brains. Now I've seen men who seemed to be the sweetest people imaginable with their friends – the very epitome of reason, kindness and charm. Their faces seem to be a guarantee for all their good qualities. 'Monsieur So-and-So – looks a real gentleman – kind, reasonable . . .' People used to say that about Ergaste. 'And so he is,' the others would reply. I've even said it so myself, 'You can see it in his honest face.' Well, you can believe that 'honest' face if you want. But a quarter of an hour later in private it all disappears and is replaced with a brutal, barbarous brooding look, which strikes terror through the whole of his household. Ergaste is married. His wife, his children, and his servants only see this ugly face, while wherever he goes in public he displays his charming look – it's like a mask he puts on whenever he goes out of the house . . . And then

there's Leandre. Aren't people delighted to see him now? Well – let me tell you something – at home he is absolutely silent, he never laughs or scolds. He is a cold, solitary and unapproachable soul. His wife scarcely knows him, his mind is a closed book to her. She is married to a shadow who emerges from his study to come to table, and then with his chilling apathy and dullness he makes them all die of boredom. Now isn't that an amusing husband! . . . Oh yes, and let's not forget Tesandre. The other day he just had a row with his wife. I arrive. I am announced. I see a man coming towards me with open arms, relaxed and as calm as can be. You'd have thought he'd just come from some witty little *tête-à-tête*. His eyes and mouth all smiles. The traitor! That's what men are like. Now who would possibly think to take pity on his wife? I found her utterly despondent, her face ashen, her eyes puffy with tears. I found her as I might well be myself one day. She was a portrait of what my future holds. But I'm not going to let myself become a copy of her. I pitied her, Lisette. And what if you should come to pity me? It would be awful, wouldn't it? Now just think what a husband can be!

COMMENTARY: Marivaux's *The Game of Love and Chance* is a prose comedy that focuses on the love affair between Silvia and Dorante. Although their impending marriage is an arranged one, they are given wide latitude by their parents to decide whether the choice is right for them. Each character decides independently to adopt a disguise as a servant in order to observe the other at close range. In disguise they find themselves attracted to each other and end up together by the end of the play. Within this simple framework Marivaux creates an intensely philosophical comedy carried along by the sparkling, cerebral dialogue. Appearance and reality become his primary themes.

Silvia, although unmarried, has a wisdom that surpasses her youth and she seems almost middle-aged in her understanding of the marriage game. She is a realist and not a romantic, she analyses rather than sentimentalises what love can be. What she sees, hears and notes in relationships has a searing quality: a puffy eye can tell her everything she needs to know. The actor has to decide how much of this is cynicism and how much is fresh-faced honesty. Silvia has standards and values that must be met. She is superb at mimicking others and at extracting small tell-tale signs of behaviour. Above all the 'temper' and temperature of a relationship must be assessed before going further. She must be played as a wholly independent woman with a mind of her own. In its time this play was quite radical because it gave characters like Silvia choice and free will. Dorante just happens to be a perfect match, but Silvia's scepticism must put him to the test before she will stamp him as acceptable. You might also note that Silvia does not find it easy to express feelings. There is something cool, detached and cautiously watchful about her.

The Country Wife
(1675) William Wycherley

Act 4, scene 1. London. A room in Pinchwife's house.

Margery Pinchwife (20s), the naïve country-born wife of the old and jealous Mr Pinchwife, has recently been brought to London by her new husband who is determined to protect her from the rakes of the town. Horner, the most ingenious of these, after seeing Margery plans to conquer her. She has been forced by her husband to write Horner a dismissive letter. Once her husband leaves the room she makes amends by penning this letter instead.

MRS PINCHWIFE.
For Mr Horner – So, I am glad he has told me his name; Dear Mr Horner, but why should I send thee such a letter, that will vex thee, and make thee angry with me; – well I will not send it – Ay but then my husband will kill me – for I see plainly, he won't let me love Mr Horner – but what care I for my husband – I won't so I won't send poor Mr Horner such a letter – but then my husband – But oh – what if I writ at bottom, my husband made me write it – Ay but then my husband wou'd see't – Can one have no shift,[1] ah, a London woman wou'd have had a hundred presently; stay – what if I shou'd write a letter, and wrap it up like this, and write upon't too; ay but then my husband wou'd see't – I don't know what to do – But yet y vads[2] I'll try, so I will – for I will not send this letter to poor Mr Horner, come what will on't.

Dear, Sweet Mr Horner – So – (*She writes and repeats what she hath writ.*) my husband wou'd have me send you a

[1] **shift** stratagem
[2] **y vads** in faith

base, rude, unmannerly letter – but I won't – *so* – and wou'd have me forbid you loving me – but I won't – *so* – and wou'd have me say to you, I hate you poor Mr Horner – but I won't tell a lie for him – *there* – for I'm sure if you and I were in the country at cards together, – *so* – I cou'd not help treading on your toe under the table – *so* – or rubbing knees with you, and staring in your face, 'till you saw me – *very well* – and then looking down, and blushing for an hour together – *so* – but I must make haste before my husband come; and now he has taught me to write letters: You shall have longer ones from me, who am

Dear, dear, poor dear Mr Horner, your most

Humble friend, and servant to command

'till death, Margery Pinchwife.

Stay I must give him a hint at bottom – *so* – now wrap it up just like t'other – *so* – now write for Mr Horner, – But oh now what shall I do with it? for here comes my husband.

Enter Pinchwife.

COMMENTARY: Wycherley's *The Country Wife* was written at a time when love and wenching were the business of comedy. It concerns Horner, a libertine, who pretends to be impotent in order to divest suspicious husbands of their wives. It seems that every female in London is willing to be seduced by Horner, even the naïve country wife of Mr Pinchwife. The action is full of licentious moments and frank talk about sex and seduction. The play also pits the manners of the city against those of the country.

Margery Pinchwife is a delightful invention and one of the great female characters of the Restoration stage. She is an equal mix of naïvety and curiosity. Once she is thrown in Horner's way she is eager to get involved. She sees nothing wrong with having an affair. Her husband Mr Pinchwife is insane with jealousy and suspicious of her every move. Once given a short leash of freedom she extends it all the way until she liberates herself from her husband's obsessions. Her letter is a wonderful acting bit; she thinks and writes, writes and thinks, all at the same time, punctuating sentences with her spoken '*so*'s. Her first letter was dictated by her husband in the scene just before this one. But this letter is entirely in her own hand. One of the endearing things about this character is that she cannot tell a lie. Another is her frank curiosity about sex. She takes to the city and city manners like a duck to water. You can see here how quickly she takes to letter-writing once she learns the basics. Although extremely simple as a person Margery is an instinctive seductress; she knows how to flatter and to flirt. Notice that she is a quick learner and everything she does has an instant facility. Although she should be played as naïve, she should not be played as either slow or stupid. Notice the repetitious use of 'so' as a kind of verbal punctuation mark for each of her sentence fragments.

The Rover (Part 1)
(1678) Aphra Behn

Act 1, scene 1. Naples at carnival time. A chamber.

Hellena (16–18), 'a gay young woman designed for a nun,' talks to her sister Florinda about love and lovers. She is curious to know about both. Hellena is wild and impulsive and not at all prepared to live the chaste life that has been chosen for her.

HELLENA.
'Tis true, I was never a lover yet – but I begin to have a shrewd guess, what 'tis to be so, and fancy it very pretty to sigh, and sing, and blush and wish, and dream and wish, and long and wish to see the man; and when I do, look pale and tremble; just as you did when my brother brought home the fine English Colonel to see you – what do you call him? Don Belvile . . . That blush betrays you – I am sure 'tis so – or is it Don Antonio the Viceroy's son – or perhaps the rich old Don Vincentio, whom my father designs for your husband? – Why do you blush again? . . . Now hang me, if I don't love thee for that dear disobedience. I love mischief strangely,[1] as most of our sex do, who are come to love nothing else – But tell me, dear Florinda, don't you love that fine *Anglese*? – for I vow next to loving him my self 'twill please me most that you do so, for he is so gay and so handsome . . . And dost thou think that ever I'll be a nun? Or[2] at least till I'm so old, I'm fit for nothing else. Faith no, Sister; and that which makes me long to know whether you love Belvile, is because I hope he has some mad companion

---

[1] **strangely** to an exceptional degree
[2] **Or** before

or other, that will spoil my devotion; nay I'm resolv'd to provide my self this Carnival, if there be e'er a handsome fellow of my humour above ground, tho I ask first. . . . Now you have provided your self with a man, you take no care for poor me – Prithee tell me, what dost thou see about me that is unfit for love – have not I a world of youth? a humour gay? a beauty passable? a vigour desirable? well shap'd? clean limb'd? sweet breath'd? and sense enough to know how all these ought to be employ'd to the best advantage: yes, I do and will. Therefore lay aside your hopes of my fortune, by my being a devotee, and tell me how you came acquainted with this Belvile; for I perceive you knew him before he came to Naples.

COMMENTARY: Behn's *The Rover*, the most popular of her plays, is a swashbuckling Restoration comedy set far from the drawing-rooms of London society. Its morality is loose and effervescent and its characters have a freedom of mind and movement which allows them to get involved in the most complex of arrangements and affairs. The plot of the play revolves around love affairs and disguises and owes a good deal to Shakespeare's romantic comedies, such as *As You Like It*. Behn's female characters have a playfulness, independence and sexual confidence that is different from their male counterparts. It is inevitable that Hellena will be a match for, and end up with, the rakish Wilmore.

Hellena's speech made up of sections from her dialogue with her sister Florinda shows what an exuberant character she is. She is witty, mischievous, curious, probing and not at all the type of young lady prepared to take vows of chastity. She is exploding with curiosity about love and the opposite sex and is also assured about her own physical attractiveness. She pesters her sister for information. You can imagine her constantly on the move as she speaks; she is a very physical character who uses language in a physical way. The actor must remember that the events of the play happen during carnival time when excitement and sexual attraction are at a peak. The world is turned topsy-turvy and women have the licence to be as licentious as men. So much of Hellena's boldness comes out of this impulsiveness. Notice how she uses sparky words and a quick-spirited sentence construction. These help the actor to give the speech the feeling that it is being improvised on the spot.

The Lucky Chance
(1686) Aphra Behn

Act 2, scene 1. London. Gayman's lodging.

Landlady (40s), Gammer Grime, enters Gayman's lodgings looking for her back rent. Gayman is a gentleman, a 'spark of the town', who is in terrible financial straits. His last hope is that he can induce his landlady, who he cannot abide, to front him yet more money. She, however, has come in search of the considerable sum of money he owes her.

LANDLADY.
More of your Money and less of your Civility, good Mr Wasteall. . . . Dear me no dears, Sir, but let me have my money – Eight weeks rent last Friday; besides taverns, ale-houses, chandlers,[1] laundresses' scores,[2] and ready money out of my purse; you know it, Sir . . . My husband! what, do you think to fright me with my Husband? – I'd have you to know I'm an honest Woman, and care not this – for my Husband. Is this all the thanks I have for my kindness, for patching, borrowing and shifting for you; 'twas but last Week I pawn'd my best petticoat, as I hope to wear it again, it cost me six and twenty shillings besides making; then this morning my new Norwich Mantua[3] followed, and two postle spoons,[4] I had the whole dozen when you came first; but they dropt, and dropt, till I had only Judas left for my Husband. . . . Then I've past my

[1] **chandlers** dealers in candles, oil and soap
[2] **scores** bills
[3] **Norwich Mantua** gown made of woven silk from Norwich
[4] **postle spoons** apostle spoons (set of twelve teaspoons with figures of the apostles on the handles)

word at the George tavern for forty shillings for you, ten shillings at my neighbour Squabs for ale, besides seven shillings to Mother Suds for washing; and do you fob me off with my husband? . . . Patience! I scorn your words, Sir – is this a place to trust in? tell me of patience, that us'd to have my money before hand; come, come, pay me quickly – or old Gregory Grimes house shall be too hot to hold you . . . No, Sir, you had good clothes when you came first, but they dwindled daily, till they dwindled to this old campaign[5] – with tan'd coloured lining – once red – but now all colours of the rainbow, a cloak to sculk in a nights, and a pair of piss-burn'd shammy breeches. Nay, your very badge of manhood's gone too. . . . Your silver sword I mean – transmogrified to the two-handed basket hilt – this old Sir Guy of Warwick[6] – which will sell for nothing but old iron. In fine[7] I'll have my money, Sir, or i'faith, Alsatia[8] shall not shelter you.

COMMENTARY: Behn's *The Lucky Chance* is a city comedy that pits youth against age. Two bustling plots follow the rivalries and schemes of young lovers and old husbands in pursuit of the same mistresses. It reveals a society in which lust and greed fight against love and penury. There is plenty of farcical action as the various plots are hastily drawn together in the final act which reveals the triumph of true love.

Gammer Grime is everything her name implies – 'a sight of her is a vomit, but he's a bold hero that dares venture on her for a kiss, and all beyond that sure is hell itself' – a disreputable landlady herself, she caters to some of the most disreputable lodgers in London. She is a distant relative of Mistress Quickly in Shakespeare's Falstaff plays. Her 'monologue' is made up of

[5] **campaign** a lined gown
[6] **Sir Guy of Warwick** slang name for a rapier
[7] **In fine** to conclude
[8] **Alsatia** a district in the city of London inhabited by criminals and debtors

replies to Gayman's interjections and it comes out in one full stream. It is clear that she has been charmed by Gayman in the past but now demands restitution. It is a richly comic speech full of details and colloquial phrases, containing a wonderful attack on Gayman's manhood. She is colourfully off-colour and creates a rising crescendo of reproach. Although a caricature who makes a brief appearance, she must create a rich and vivid impression during the few minutes she is on stage. She has obviously been susceptible to Gayman's charms before and is considerably out of pocket as a result. The actor must play her as fighting against succumbing to his charms and his offers of wine. She is trying to hold her ground against this practised seducer who knows exactly how to get what he wants.

The Relapse
(1696) Sir John Vanbrugh

Act 5, scene 4. London. A drawing-room.

Amanda (20s) is married to Loveless. Prior to the beginning of the play Loveless had abandoned Amanda and England so as to escape his debts. On his return she has been endlessly forgiving of his ways, but here she confronts her suspicions of his new deceitfulness or 'relapse' into the errors of his old ways. She has just returned home from Whitehall where, in disguise, she has seen her husband rendez-vous with his lover.

AMANDA.
At last I am convinced. My eyes are testimonies
Of his falsehood. The base, ungrateful, perjured villain –
Good gods – What slippery stuff are men composed of?
Sure, the account of their creation's false,
And 'twas the woman's rib that they were formed of;
But why am I thus angry?
This poor relapse should only move my scorn.
'Tis true: the roving flights of his unfinished youth,
Had strong excuse, from the plea of nature;
Reason had thrown the reins loose on his neck,
And slipped him to unlimited desire.
If therefore he went wrong, he had a claim
To my forgiveness, and I did him right.
But since the years of manhood, rein him in,
And reason well digested into thought,
Has pointed out the course he ought to run;
If now he strays?
'Twould be as weak, and mean in me to pardon,
As it has been in him t'offend.

But hold:
'Tis an ill cause indeed, where nothing's to be said for't.
My beauty possibly is in the wane;
Perhaps sixteen has greater charms for him:
Yes, there's the secret: but let him know,
My quiver's not entirely emptied yet,
I still have darts, and I can shoot 'em too;
They're not so blunt, but they can enter still,
The want's not in my power, but in my will.
Virtue's his friend, or through another's heart,
I yet could find the way, to make his smart.

COMMENTARY: Vanbrugh's *The Relapse, or Virtue in Danger* is a comedy that follows the fall from virtue of the character Loveless with his wife's cousin Berinthia, while his wife Amanda is being chased by Worthy, a gentleman of the town. All is righted in the end and virtue triumphs. In the sub-plot Young Fashion schemes to cheat his older brother Lord Foppington out of his intended bride, Miss Hoyden, a naïve country heiress who is the daughter of Sir Tunbelly Clumsy. Lord Foppington also goes in pursuit of Amanda at one point. The play is a comic delight largely because of the rich characterisations and the sudden twists and turns of the plot.

Amanda comes into this scene in a furious state, having just dismissed her maid. She has seen her husband in the park with another woman, not yet realising that it is her cousin Berinthia. The entire soliloquy is written in the blank verse which Vanbrugh resorted to for emotional speeches like this one; however, the language is quite natural and too poetic a delivery should be avoided. Think of each line as a separate thought and move through the monologue as if across a series of stepping stones; this will make it easier to memorise and then to perform. This speech is also one in which a character grows through a process of enlightenment ('My eyes are testimonies / Of his falsehood.') After attacking her husband she then stops short ('But hold:') and turns to self-criticism, before resolving to fight on. It is best to make the speech not comic but real so that the character's resentment and sense of rejection are strongly apparent. Notice how much Amanda worries about her age.

The Provok'd Wife
(1697) Sir John Vanbrugh

Act 1, scene 1. London. A room in Sir John Brute's house.

Lady Brute (20s), wife of Sir John Brute, can no longer stand the idea of being married. She is an elegant, put-upon lady who finds herself, after two years of marriage, in an impossible situation. This is what provokes her. The play opens with an argument between her and Sir John and he has just left the stage in a huff.

LADY BRUTE.
The devil's in the fellow I think – I was told before I married him, that thus 'twould be; but I thought I had charms enough to govern him; and that where there was an estate, a woman must needs be happy; so my vanity has deceived me, and my ambition has made me uneasy. But some comfort still; if one would be revenged of him, these are good times; a woman may have a gallant, and a separate maintenance[1] too – The surly puppy – yet he's a fool for't: for hitherto he has been no monster: but who knows how far he may provoke me. I never loved him, yet I have been ever true to him; and that, in spite of all the attacks of art and nature upon a poor weak woman's heart, in favour of a tempting lover. Methinks so noble a defence as I have made, should be rewarded with a better usage – or who can tell – perhaps a good part of what I suffer from my husband may be a judgement upon me for my cruelty to my lover. – Lord with what pleasure could I indulge that thought, were there but a possibility of finding arguments to make it good.

[1] **maintenance** a woman divorced for adultery could receive alimony from her husband

86

– And how do I know but there may – Let me see – What
opposes? – My matrimonial vow? – Why, what did I vow: I
think I promised to be true to my husband. Well; and he
promised to be kind to me. But he han't kept his word –
Why then I'm absolved from mine – aye, that seems clear to
me. The argument's good between the King and the
people, why not between the husband and the wife? Oh,
but that condition was not expressed. – No matter, 'twas
understood. Well, by all I see, if I argue the matter a little
longer with myself, I shan't find so many bugbears in the
way, as I thought I should. Lord what fine notions of virtue
do we women take up upon the credit of old foolish
philosophers. Virtue's its own reward, virtue's this, virtue's
that; – virtue's an ass, and a gallant's worth forty on't.

COMMENTARY: Vanbrugh's *The Provok'd Wife* revolves around
the unsatisfactory marriage of Sir John and Lady Brute which
must continue because a divorce is not possible. The institution of
marriage becomes a ripe comic target in the form of various
adulterous liaisons. Lady Brute encourages the attentions of her
admirer Constant and becomes involved in a series of compromis-
ing affairs which lead to nothing in the end. A host of romantic
sub-plots keeps the action on the level of farce.

Lady Brute and her husband Sir John have just had a
matrimonial row sparked off by Lady Brute's simply enquiring if
Sir John will be dining at home or away. This was sufficient to
send Sir John off into a tirade against his wife and the restrictions
of married life, concluding with his regret that he had ever
married her. Lady Brute in a vengeful and despairing mood
convinces herself that she has no obligations in her marriage and
is free to do and love as she pleases. In the world of this play
'rows' and 'vows' create tension. Lady Brute begins to scheme
about a way of getting out of this marriage profitably: with money
and a new 'gallant'. There is a good deal of reality about her and
she is not given to simpering weakness when faced with an
obstacle like Sir John. She is truly a woman 'provok'd' and rather
than defeat her it sets her thinking. The part of the monologue,

set off by dashes, shows that process at work. The actor really must make the fragments become the separate parts of a plan knitting themselves together. She is looking for a legal way out of the marriage contract and appears here like a lawyer preparing her evidence for prosecution, assembling all the facts before taking action.

The Way of the World
(1700) William Congreve

Act 4, scene 1. A room in Lady Wishfort's house.

Lady Wishfort (50s) is awaiting the arrival of Sir Rowland, the wealthy country uncle of Mirabell. She hopes to marry him. Her maid Foible, however, has conspired with Mirabell to pass off her servant Waitwell as Sir Rowland. Here Lady Wishfort is in a frenzy of anticipation and is speaking to Foible.

LADY WISHFORT.
Is Sir Rowland coming, say'st thou, Foible? and are things in order? . . . Have you pulvilled[1] the coachman and postilion that they may not stink of the stable when Sir Rowland comes by? . . . And are the dancers and the music ready, that he may be entertained in all points with correspondence to his passion? . . . And – well – and how do I look Foible?

[FOIBLE. Most killing well, madam.]

Well, and how shall I receive him? in what figure shall I give his heart the first impression? there is a great deal in the first impression. Shall I sit? – no, I won't sit – I'll walk – ay, I'll walk from the door upon his entrance; and then turn full upon him – no, that will be too sudden. I'll lie, – ay, I'll lie down – I'll receive him in my little dressing-room, there's a couch – yes, yes, I'll give the first impression on a couch. – I won't lie neither, but loll and lean upon one elbow: with one foot a little dangling off, jogging in a thoughtful way – yes – and then as soon as he appears, start,

---

[1] **pulvilled** dusted with scented powder

ay, start and be surprised, and rise to meet him in a pretty disorder – yes – O, nothing is more alluring than a levee[2] from a couch, in some confusion: it shows the foot to advantage, and furnishes with blushes, and recomposing airs beyond comparison. Hark! there's a coach.

COMMENTARY: In Congreve's *The Way of the World* the plot concerns the efforts of Mirabell to marry Millamant, despite the obstruction of her aunt Lady Wishfort to whom he has feigned attraction in order to disguise his suit for Millamant. Lady Wishfort is the guardian of the property he desires. Congreve's play is full of brilliant scenes, sparkling dialogue and lifelike characterisations. It should be acted as realistically as possible without any affected or caricatured mannerisms whatsoever. The dialogue and needs of the characters should feel contemporary and not antique.

Lady Wishfort is a terrible snob, and a vain conceited woman whose looks are dwindling ('I am errantly flayed – I look like an old peeled wall. Thou must repair me Foible, before Sir Rowland comes, or I shall never keep up to my picture.') Throughout the play we see this aged coquette at her toilette, trying cosmetically to counter the ravages of time. The actor should realise that Lady Wishfort spends her time trying to fulfil her wishes to be youthful again and be beloved by a man. She is also one of the most artificial and unnatural characters in the play. In this monologue she is trying to stage-manage a seduction and anticipate the reactions of her gentleman caller. Notice how she is in a flurry of activity, rehearsing for her starring performance. She checks her costume, her set, her blocking, her ankle, her blushes, etc., using Foible as her stand-in audience. She is staging a scene that will show her to best advantage. Although the speech may seem rushed it would be good to take your time and enjoy the elaboration on verbal and physical detail, especially the foot.

---

[2] **levee** a rising (derived from a ritual at which the French court would attend the ceremonial rising of the king each morning)

The Way of the World
(1700) William Congreve

Act 4, scene 1. London. A room in Lady Wishfort's town house.

Mrs[1] Millamant (20s) is a fine society lady. She is strong-willed, observant, witty and thoroughly schooled in 'the way of the world'. Throughout the play she is being pursued and wooed by Edward Mirabell. In this moment Millamant tells Mirabell the conditions under which she will contemplate and tolerate his proposal of marriage.

MRS MILLAMANT.

Ah! I'll never marry, unless I am first made sure of my will and pleasure. . . . My dear liberty, shall I leave thee? My faithful solitude, my darling contemplation, must I bid you then adieu? Ay-h adieu – my morning thoughts, agreeable wakings, indolent slumbers, all *ye douceurs, ye sommeils du matin*[2] adieu? – I can't do't 'tis more than impossible – positively, Mirabell, I'll lie abed in a morning as long as I please. . . . And d'ye hear, I won't be called names after I'm married; positively I won't be called names. . . . Aye, as wife, spouse, my dear, joy, jewel, love, sweetheart, and the rest of that nauseous cant, in which men and their wives are so fulsomely familiar – I shall never bear that – good Mirabell, don't let us be familiar or fond, nor kiss before folks, like my Lady Fadler and Sir Francis: nor go to Hyde Park together the first Sunday in a new chariot, to provoke eyes and whispers, and then never to be seen there together

[1] **Mrs** in Congreve's time the designation Mrs was used for both married and unmarried women

[2] **ye douceurs . . . matin** sweetnesses and morning naps

again; as if we were proud of one another the first week, and ashamed of one another ever after. Let us never visit together, nor go to a play together; but let us be very strange[3] and well-bred: let us be as strange as if we had been married a great while; and as well bred as if we were not married at all. . . . Trifles! – As liberty to pay and receive visits to and from whom I please; to write and receive letters, without interrogatories or wry faces on your part; to wear what I please; and choose conversation with regard only to my own taste; to have no obligation upon me to converse with wits that I don't like, because they are your acquaintance: or to be intimate with fools, because they may be your relations. Come to dinner when I please; dine in my dressing-room when I'm out of humour, without giving a reason. To have my closet[4] inviolate; to be sole empress of my tea-table, which you must never presume to approach without first asking leave. And lastly, wherever I am, you shall always knock at the door before you come in. These articles subscribed, if I continue to endure you a little longer, I may by degrees dwindle into a wife.

COMMENTARY: The intricate plot of *The Way of the World* partly revolves around the attempts of the urbane and witty Mirabell to marry the equally sophisticated and quick-witted Millamant. Their world is the insulated one of stylish high society with a strict set of codes and manners. Property and keeping property are a central concern. Characters use language in an ironic and complex way both as an offensive and defensive weapon that maps out the ownership of space and keeps emotion under wraps. Congreve's play is full of brilliant scenes, sparkling dialogue and lifelike characterisations. It should be acted as realistically as possible without any affected or caricatured

[3] **strange** reserved
[4] **closet** boudoir or private sitting-room

mannerisms whatsoever. The dialogue and needs of the characters should feel contemporary and not antique.

Act Four of the drama contains the famous 'bargaining' scene in which Millamant and Mirabell agree to marry after negotiating an intricate verbal contract setting forth the various rights and responsibilities of one towards the other. The language of this monologue must be performed with these legalistic intentions in mind. Notice that this is not a speech about love. At no point does she declare herself or reveal her affections for Mirabell. In other words this speech is not all sweetness and light but contains provisos and warnings. Millamant really does seem like a lawyer dictating terms under which she will cohabit and 'by degrees dwindle into a wife'. What she is preserving are her privacy and independence. The wit and fun in the speech come of their own accord and should not be forced in performance. The actor should play an ingenious woman and let the intelligence of the character speak for itself.

The Beaux' Stratagem
(1707) George Farquhar

Act 2, scene 1. A gallery in Lady Bountiful's country house.

Mrs Sullen (20s) is married to Lady Bountiful's son Sullen, 'a country blockhead brutal to his wife'. Here she talks to her sister-in-law Dorinda about the woes of married life and warns her to avoid a man like Sullen.

MRS SULLEN.

O, sister, sister, if ever you marry, beware of a sullen, silent sot, one that's always musing but never thinks. There's some diversion in a talking blockhead, and since a woman must wear chains, I would have the pleasure of hearing 'em rattle a little. Now you shall see, but take this by the way. He came home this morning at his usual hour of four, wakened me out of a sweet dream of something else by tumbling over the tea table, which he broke all to pieces. After his man and he had rolled about the room like sick passengers in a storm, he comes flounce into bed, dead as a salmon into a fishmonger's basket, his feet cold as ice, his breath hot as a furnace and his hands and his face as greasy as his flannel nightcap. Oh matrimony! He tosses up the clothes[1] with a barbarous swing over his shoulders, disorders the whole economy[2] of my bed, leaves me half naked, and my whole night's comfort is the tuneable serenade of that wakeful nightingale – his nose. O, the pleasure of counting the melancholy clock by a snoring husband! But now, sister, you shall see how handsomely, being a well-bred man, he will beg my pardon.

[1] **clothes** bedclothes
[2] **economy** organisation

COMMENTARY: Farquhar's *The Beaux' Stratagem* is a comedy about love on all different levels. Thomas Aimwell and his friend Archer, the two 'beaux', have just arrived at the local inn in the provincial town of Litchfield. They hope to better their fortunes and learn about the family that resides at the nearby manor house. This includes Lady Bountiful; her unmarried daughter Dorinda; her ill-tempered son Sullen; and his discontented wife Mrs Sullen. Their involvement with this family leads to unending complications before the untangling at the end in which Archer and Mrs Sullen actually end up as a couple.

Mrs Sullen lives a life of romantic hardship and marital bondage which she groans and moans about every chance she gets. Once the dreadful Sullen appears you can appreciate her plight. From morning to night and even on Sundays he is continually drunk. She is so detailed about her drunken husband coming to bed that the actor must feel that she has been through this scenario time and time again. Notice how simple and specific each of her images is, i.e. 'he comes flounce into bed, dead as a salmon into a fishmonger's basket . . .' One never has to stop to think about what she means. It is clear that she lives and shares a bed with a completely thoughtless lout who just takes her for granted. Even the snoring is etched in detail. Mrs Sullen comes from the sophisticated city and is despairing in the country. This is as inappropriate a marriage as you can imagine; one based on money not love. As soon as she has spoken Sullen enters and we see exactly what she has been talking about. Her words of warning are made flesh. Use the speech as a kind of vivid introduction to a character who will soon enter.

The Rivals

(1775) Richard Brinsley Sheridan

Act 1, scene 2. Bath. A dressing-room in Mrs Malaprop's lodgings.

Mrs Malaprop (40s) is talking to Sir Anthony Absolute about the pros and cons of education for women. She hopes to arrange a marriage between Sir Anthony's son Captain Absolute and her wealthy niece and ward Lydia Languish. She thinks herself 'queen of the dictionary'.

MRS MALAPROP.

Observe me, Sir Anthony. I would by no means wish a daughter of mine to be a progeny[1] of learning; I don't think so much learning becomes a young woman; for instance – I would never let her meddle with Greek, or Hebrew, or Algebra, or Simony,[2] or Fluxions,[3] or Paradoxes,[4] or such inflammatory branches of learning – neither would it be necessary for her to handle any of your mathematical, astronomical, diabolical instruments. But, Sir Anthony, I would send her, at nine years old, to a boarding-school, in order to learn a little ingenuity and artifice. Then, Sir, she should have a supercilious[5] knowledge in accounts; and as she grew up, I would have her instructed in geometry,[6] that she might know something of the contagious[7] countries;

---

[1] **progeny** offspring: for 'prodigy'
[2] **Simony** the crime of selling or buying church offices: for 'cyclometry?' or 'ciphering'?
[3] **Fluxions** Newtonian calculus
[4] **Paradoxes** for 'parallaxes'? (an astronomical term)
[5] **supercilious** for 'superficial'
[6] **geometry** for 'geography'
[7] **contagious** for 'contiguous'

but above all, Sir Anthony, she should be mistress of orthodoxy,[8] that she might not mis-spell, and mis-pronounce words so shamefully as girls usually do; and likewise that she might reprehend[9] the true meaning of what she is saying. This, Sir Anthony, is what I would have a woman know; and I don't think there is a superstitious[10] article in it.

COMMENTARY: Sheridan's *The Rivals* is a comedy of intrigue and mistaken identity. Sir Anthony Absolute wants his son Captain Absolute to marry the wealthy heiress Lydia Languish. He is unaware that Captain Absolute is already wooing Lydia disguised as the dashing Ensign Beverley, a role he has adopted to fulfil Lydia's romantic notions of elopement. Lydia's aunt Mrs Malaprop disapproves of the poor Beverley and threatens to disinherit Lydia if she marries him rather than Captain Absolute. A further sub-plot involves Absolute's friend Bob Acre who is also in love with Lydia and challenges Beverley to a duel. All is straightened out in the end after much complication.

Mrs Malaprop is one of the great comic characters of English drama. Her misuse of words and their meanings has given us the term 'malapropism' (from the French *mal à propos* or 'out of place'). Going through this speech you will encounter over a dozen of them. Her monologue is a minefield of blunders which she handles with her patented *savoir faire*. Never let the lady-like guise drop for a moment. Some of the meanings she intends are not even clear but the actor must speak them with assurance as though the meaning is perfectly clear: never telegraph the fact that you are using language inappropriately. She is the invention of an age which was making radical headway in the natural sciences and linguistics; these are the two main themes she seizes on for her misapplied summary of the ideal education for a young lady. Mrs Malaprop is a proud woman whose position and wealth give her great assurance.

[8] **orthodoxy** for 'orthography' (correct or conventional spelling)
[9] **reprehend** for 'comprehend'
[10] **superstitious** for 'superfluous'

The Rivals
(1775) Richard Brinsley Sheridan

Act 5, scene 1. Bath. Julia's dressing-room in her lodgings.

Lydia Languish (18–20) is a wealthy heiress. Her aunt Mrs Malaprop has been trying to arrange a marriage between Lydia and Captain John Absolute, Sir Anthony Absolute's son. Lydia has favoured instead the penniless Ensign Beverley. However, she has been outraged to discover that her beloved Beverley has been deceiving her all along and is, in fact, none other than Captain John Absolute. She has come to visit her friend Julia to vent her anger and frustration only to find out that Julia already knows about the deception.

LYDIA.
So, then, I see I have been deceived by everyone! – but I don't care – I'll never have him. . . . Why, is it not provoking; when I thought we were coming to the prettiest distress imaginable, to find myself made a mere Smithfield bargain[1] of at last. – There had I projected one of the most sentimental elopements! – so becoming a disguise! – so amiable a ladder of ropes! – conscious[2] moon – four horses – Scotch parson[3] – with such surprise to Mrs Malaprop – and such paragraphs in the newspapers! – Oh, I shall die with disappointment. . . . Now – sad reverse! – what have I to expect, but, after a deal of flimsy preparation with a bishop's licence,[4] and my aunt's blessing, to go simpering

---

[1] **Smithfield bargain** a sharp bargain, here a marriage made for money
[2] **conscious** sharing in human feelings
[3] **Scotch parson** People under twenty-one were not legally allowed to marry without their parents' consent. No such law applied in Scotland and it was therefore a popular destination for eloping couples.
[4] **bishop's licence** This gave permission for a marriage to take place in the church of the parish in which one of the parties lived.

up to the altar; or perhaps be cried three times[5] in a country church, and have an unmannerly fat clerk ask the consent of every butcher in the parish to join John Asbolute and Lydia Languish, *spinster*! Oh, that I should live to hear myself called spinster! . . . How mortifying, to remember the dear delicious shifts[6] I used to be put to, to gain half a minute's conversation with this fellow! How often have I stole forth, in the coldest night in January, and found him in the garden, stuck like a dripping statue! There would he kneel to me in the snow, and sneeze and cough so pathetically! he shivering with cold, and I with apprehension! and while the freezing blast numbed our joints, how warmly would he press me to pity his flame, and glow with mutual ardour! – Ah, Julia! that was something like being in love.

COMMENTARY: Sheridan's *The Rivals* is a comedy of intrigue and mistaken identity. Sir Anthony Absolute wants his son Captain Absolute to marry the wealthy heiress Lydia Languish. He is unaware that Captain Absolute is already wooing Lydia disguised as the dashing Ensign Beverley, a role he has adopted to fulfil Lydia's romantic illusions of love and elopement. Lydia's aunt Mrs Malaprop disapproves of the poor Beverley and threatens to disinherit Lydia if she marries him rather than Captain Absolute. A second sub-plot involves the sentimental pair of lovers Faulkland and Julia Melville. All is straightened out in the end after much complication, farce, and comic anguish.

Lydia Languish is appropriately named. She wants to escape reality and 'languish' in a world ruled by sentiment and populated by brave, penniless and handsome lovers who will kneel at her feet. She is addicted to sentimental fiction and wants her world to mirror the one she reads about in the pages of romantic novels. Her anger in this scene comes from the fact that her dream bubble has been burst. Captain Absolute and Ensign Beverley are the

[5] **cried three times** The banns would have to be cried on three successive Sundays in the selected church.
[6] **shifts** contrivances

same man, though Lydia clearly will only ever consider her fantasy man as the 'real one'. When you look at the speech you can see just how far advanced her plans were. She has created a whole elopement scenario which has suffered a 'sad reverse'. The reality she now fantasises about is at the opposite pole even though it too is a fantasy of a different sort. Lydia is a long way from ever becoming a spinster. She is, however, a prisoner of the elaborate fictions she sees in her mind. Love to her is not a tested and tried proposition but something in the realm of illusion. The comedy in the speech derives in part from Lydia's severe disappointment and that is something the actor should play straight. It is a bit like arriving at the church on your wedding day and finding the groom has backed out. But you can signal that it has all been an elaborate joke.

Lady Windermere's Fan
(1892) Oscar Wilde

Act 1. London. Morning-room in Lord Windermere's house.

The Duchess of Berwick (40s) pays a social call on Lady Windermere. Her real aim is to leave behind a nasty piece of gossip concerning Lord Windermere and the notorious Mrs Erlynne. She edges up to the subject until Lady Windermere challenges her with, 'My husband – what has he got to do with any woman of that kind?' This is just the invitation the Duchess has been waiting for.

DUCHESS OF BERWICK.
Ah, what indeed, dear? That is the point. He goes to see her continually, and stops for hours at a time, and while he is there she is not at home to any one. Not that many ladies call on her, dear, but she has a great many disreputable men friends – my own brother particularly, as I told you – and that is what makes it so dreadful about Windermere. We looked upon *him* as being such a model husband, but I am afraid there is no doubt about it. My dear nieces – you know the Saville girls, don't you? – such nice domestic creatures – plain, dreadfully plain, but so good – well, they're always at the window doing fancy work, and making ugly things for the poor, which I think so useful of them in these dreadful socialistic days, and this terrible woman has taken a house in Curzon Street, right opposite them – such a respectable street, too! I don't know what we're coming to! And they tell me that Windermere goes there four and five times a week – they *see* him. They can't help it – and although they never talk scandal, they – well, of course – they remark on it to every one. And the worst of it all is that I have been told that this woman has got a great deal of money out of

somebody, for it seems that she came to London six months ago without anything at all to speak of, and now she has this charming house in Mayfair, drives her ponies in the Park every afternoon and all – well, all – since she has known poor dear Windermere.

[LADY WINDERMERE. Oh, I can't believe it!]

But it's quite true, my dear. The whole of London knows it. That is why I felt it was better to come and talk to you, and advise you to take Windermere away at once to Homburg or to Aix, where he'll have something to amuse him, and where you can watch him all day long. I assure you, my dear, that on several occasions after I was first married, I had to pretend to be very ill, and was obliged to drink the most unpleasant mineral waters, merely to get Berwick out of town. He was so extremely susceptible. Though I am bound to say he never gave away any large sums of money to anybody. He is far too high-principled for that!

COMMENTARY: Wilde's *Lady Windermere's Fan* is a comedy of manners that pits romance against intrigue. A dropped fan becomes the crucial piece of evidence in this 'well-made play'. Hurt and upset that her husband is showing interest in Mrs Erlynne, a woman of doubtful reputation, Lady Windermere decides to leave him and run off with Lord Darlington, a persistant and charming suitor. Mrs Erlynne, actually Lady Windermere's mother, deserted her husband and daughter many years earlier, before being deserted herself. She learns of Lady Windermere's rash decision – by means of a dropped note meant for Lord Windermere – and rushes to Lord Darlington's rooms. Here the main complications of the plot ensue as Mrs Erlynne works to protect Lady Windermere's reputation by claiming that Lady Windermere's incriminating fan, found in Lord Darlington's rooms, is one she had picked up at Lady Windermere's ball, casting further doubt on her own integrity. Vital reputation is preserved and the intrigue works to produce a happy conclusion.

The Duchess of Berwick makes an all-too-brief appearance in the play. Her main function is to sow instant seeds of doubt in Lady Windermere's mind as to the fidelity of her husband, and to drop well-placed clues. The Duchess is a distant relative of the tattling gossips of eighteenth-century drama. Her malice is sugar-coated and often cloaked by little diversionary side trips away from the route of the main subject. Like all gossips, she preys on the weaknesses of her victims. Lady Windermere is young and newly married so her relationship with her husband has not yet coalesced into one of mutual trust. Women like the Duchess move from morning-room to morning-room in the hope of finding just such victims and picking up more sources of scandal en route. Her wonderful nieces are part of her network of spies. Notice how she strategically places special incriminating words, especially those with a double meaning, throughout her speech: 'disreputable', 'dreadful', 'doubt', 'dear', 'respectable', 'scandal'. All of these are delicious words that the actor can really wrap her tongue around and relish. Though difficult, you must try not to play the character too broadly as a scandal-monger. She is a ridiculous woman, but a proud and dangerous one. Her title and nobility give her great licence.

A Woman of No Importance
(1893) Oscar Wilde

Act 2. The drawing-room at Hunstanton Chase. After dinner.

*Mrs Allonby (20s–30s), a sophisticated society lady, sits and talks
with Lady Stutfield and Lady Hunstanton. Earlier she was flirting
with Lord Illingworth so we can assume that she is a lady of
experience. The talk turns to men and theories about the ideal man.*

MRS ALLONBY.
The Ideal Man! Oh, the Ideal Man should talk to us as if we
were goddesses, and treat us as if we were children. He
should refuse all our serious requests, and gratify every one
of our whims. He should encourage us to have caprices, and
forbid us to have missions. He should always say much
more than he means and always mean much more than he
says. . . . He should never run down other pretty women.
That would show he had no taste, or make one suspect that
he had too much. No; he should be nice about them all, but
say that somehow they don't attract him. . . . If we ask him
a question about anything, he should give us an answer all
about ourselves. He should invariably praise us for whatever qualities he knows we haven't got. But he should be
pitiless, quite pitiless, in reproaching us for the virtues we
have never dreamed of possessing. He should never believe
that we know the use of useful things. That would be
unforgivable. But he should shower on us everything we
don't want. . . . He should persistently compromise us in
public, and treat us with absolute respect when we are
alone. And yet he should be always ready to have a perfectly
terrible scene, whenever we want one, and to become
miserable, absolutely miserable, at a moment's notice, and
104

to overwhelm us with reproaches in less than twenty minutes, and to be positively violent at the end of half an hour, and to leave us for ever at a quarter to eight, when we have to go and dress for dinner. And when, after that, one has seen him for really the last time, and he has refused to take back the little things he has given one, and promised never to communicate with one again, or to write one any foolish letters, he should be perfectly broken-hearted, and telegraph to one all day long, and send one little notes every half-hour by a private hansom, and dine quite alone at the club, so that every one should know how unhappy he was. And after a whole dreadful week, during which one has gone about everywhere with one's husband, just to show how absolutely lonely one was, he may be given a third last parting, in the evening, and then, if his conduct has been quite irreproachable, and one has behaved really badly to him, he should be allowed to admit that he has been entirely in the wrong, and when he has admitted that, it becomes a woman's duty to forgive, and one can do it all over again from the beginning, with variations.

COMMENTARY: Wilde's *A Woman of No Importance*, although a comedy, deals with serious subjects: illegitimacy and the sexual exploitation of women. Set on a country estate it focuses on class and the role of outsiders in that society. A youthful romance between Rachel Arbuthnot and George Harford (later Lord Illingworth) produced a child, Gerald Arbuthnot. Illingworth, despite having promised to marry Rachel, ignominiously abandoned her, turning his back on her and the child he has never known. This leads to Gerald becoming totally dependent on his mother and ignorant of either his origins or his true relationship to Lord Illingworth, a man who now wants to employ him as his private secretary. Illingworth himself only finds out he is Gerald's father at the climactic end of Act Three. The sins of the past now surface in the present and must be reconciled. By the close of the play the Arbuthnots turn their back on Lord Illingworth, rejecting him, his money and everything he stands for.

Mrs Allonby's speech is a treat for an actor. The path of it is so clearly laid out you have only to follow it to its delightful conclusion. The relationship it depicts is vivid and the narrative so strong that it practically acts itself. What you need here is enough breath and balance to traverse the length of the speech and remain refreshed by the end. Mrs Allonby is a consummate conversationalist, her company is adored and she is a frequent guest largely because of her beguiling wit. She is also an experienced woman with numerous affairs to draw on for her illustrations. Mrs Allonby has charm, allure, composure and sophistication. A woman 'of' importance who acts as a foil to the woman of 'no' importance, Mrs Arbuthnot. She knows how to handle men. Notice how each sentence has a perfect balance: each dip in tone is met with a rise in tone. The grace in the delivery comes from the mixing and matching of contrasts as she pits one thought against the other. The wit comes of itself and should not be forced. Try to be interesting and not merely witty.

The Second Mrs Tanqueray
(1893) Arthur Wing Pinero

Act 2. A morning-room in Aubrey Tanqueray's house,
'Highercoombe', near Willowmere, Surrey.

*Paula Tanqueray in Pinero's description is 'a young woman of about
twenty-seven; beautiful, fresh, innocent-looking.' She has recently
married Aubrey Tanqueray (42) and together they have left London to
retire to his country estate where they live with Ellean (19), his
daughter from an earlier marriage. The differences in their social
background begin to create tensions and disagreements. Paula has
started to write a letter and stops to flare up at her husband.*

PAULA (*walking away, throws letter down*).
Oh! I've no patience with you! You'll kill me with this life!
(*She crosses to back of chair, selects some flowers from a vase on
the table, cuts and arranges them and fastens them in her
bodice.*) What is my existence Sunday to Saturday? In the
morning, a drive down to the village with the groom, to give
my orders to the tradespeople. At lunch, you and Ellean.
(*Playing with nosegay off table.*) In the afternoon, a novel,
the newspapers; if fine, another drive – *if* fine! Tea – you
and Ellean. Then two hours of dusk; then dinner – you and
Ellean. Then a game of Bésique, you and I, while Ellean
reads a religious book in a dull corner. Then a yawn from
me, another from you, a sigh from Ellean; three figures
suddenly rise – 'Good night, good night, good night!'
(*Imitating a kiss.*) 'God bless you!' (*With an exaggerated sigh
of dejection and putting nosegay in belt.*) Ah! . . . (*Pointing to
the window.*) Do you believe these people will ever come
round us? Your former crony, Mrs Cortelyon? Or the grim
old vicar, or that wife of his whose huge nose is positively
indecent? Or the Ullathornes, or the Gollans, or Lady

William Petres? I know better! And when the young ones gradually take the place of the old, there will still remain the sacred tradition that the dreadful person who lives at the top of the hill is never, under any circumstances, to be called upon! (*She moves centre.*) And so we shall go on here, year in and year out, until the sap is run out of our lives, and we're stale and dry and withered from sheer, solitary respectability. Upon my word, I wonder we didn't see that we should have been far happier if we'd gone in for the devil-may-care, *café*-living sort of life in town! After all, *I* have a set and you might have joined it. It's true I did want, dearly, dearly, to be a married woman, but where's the pride in being a married woman among married women who are – married!

COMMENTARY: Pinero's *The Second Mrs Tanqueray* is a classic problem play set in the world of high society, which has a woefully unhappy ending. Paula, the heroine, is a woman with a questionable past. She marries the older, widowed Aubrey Tanqueray and retires with him to his country home, but is not accepted by his friends or by his nineteen-year-old daughter Ellean. The arrival of Ellean's suitor, one of Paula's former lovers, provokes a series of disastrous revelations and strife. The play ends with Paula's suicide.

Paula Tanqueray is trying to live up to the expectations of being Aubrey Tanqueray's 'second' wife. She is whispered about and sometimes openly insulted by Tanqueray's neighbours and associates. This snobbery, coupled with her own disreputable past, begins to have its effect. She finds life in the country boring after her exciting social life in London. Notice how repetitive and confining she finds her new life. She makes it sound like she is in prison, following a daily unvarying routine. She is also quite lonely and aware that she is not getting any younger. Ellean is a rival for Aubrey Tanqueray's affections and makes no effort to make Paula feel welcome. Paula uses all these accumulated irritations to help her stage her fit of pique. An actor should remember that Pinero loved to create details which give the performer something on which to concentrate her imagination, i.e. Paula's precise catalogue of daily rituals and her fiddling with the flowers. You can move through this speech step by step following Pinero's lead until you have created an elaborately embroidered picture of people and a social world. Pinero was also insistent that his actor move with the speech as it shifts attention, to protect her from becoming boring: notice his indications of this in the stage directions. He wanted the actor to fill the stage with her story-telling presence and keep the audience's focus on herself.

An Ideal Husband

(1895) Oscar Wilde

Act 2. London. Morning-room at Sir Robert Chiltern's house.

Mabel Chiltern (18–20s), the charming and vivacious sister of Sir Robert Chiltern, is talking to her sister-in-law Lady Gertrude Chiltern about one of her more persistent suitors, Tommy Trafford, who is Sir Robert's private secretary.

MABEL CHILTERN.

Well, Tommy has proposed to me again. Tommy really does nothing but propose to me. He proposed to me last night in the music-room, when I was quite unprotected, as there was an elaborate trio going on. I didn't dare to make the smallest repartee, I need hardly tell you. If I had, it would have stopped the music at once. Musical people are so absurdly unreasonable. They always want one to be perfectly dumb at the very moment when one is longing to be absolutely deaf. Then he proposed to me in broad daylight this morning, in front of that dreadful statue of Achilles. Really, the things that go on in front of that work of art are quite appalling. The police should interfere. At luncheon I saw by the glare in his eye that he was going to propose again, and I just managed to check him in time by assuring him that I was a bimetallist. Fortunately I don't know what bimetallism means. And I don't believe anybody else does either. But the observation crushed Tommy for ten minutes. He looked quite shocked. And then Tommy is so annoying in the way he proposes. If he proposed at the top of his voice, I should not mind so much. That might produce some effect on the public. But he does it in a horrid confidential way. When Tommy wants to be romantic he talks

110

to one just like a doctor. I am very fond of Tommy, but his methods of proposing are quite out of date. I wish, Gertrude, you would speak to him, and tell him that once a week is quite often enough to propose to any one, and that it should always be done in a manner that attracts some attention.

COMMENTARY: Wilde's *An Ideal Husband* is an ironic comedy that attacks the notion of an 'ideal' anyone. Twenty years before the start of the play, the well-regarded and morally upstanding Sir Robert Chiltern, currently an Under-Secretary for Foreign Affairs, sold classified government secrets to the unscrupulous Baron Arnheim to secure his future position and fortune. The action of the play focuses on his blackmail by Mrs Cheveley, a former lover of the Baron, who is trying to gain government influence for a project in which she is investing. The moral quandary is revealed to Sir Robert's wife Lady Gertrude Chiltern and domestic strife is the result. Love corrects the balance in the end and reputations are only bruised.

Mabel Chiltern is one of Wilde's most exquisite creations although her importance in the plot is negligible. He describes her as follows: 'the most ornamental person in London'; dressed 'in the most ravishing frock'; she doesn't like to wear pearls because they 'make one look so plain, so good, and so intellectual'; she 'is a perfect example of the English type of prettiness, the apple-blossom type. She has all the fragrance and freedom of a flower. There is ripple after ripple of sunlight in her hair, and the little mouth, with its parted lips, is expectant, like the mouth of a child. She has the fascinating tyranny of youth, and the astonishing courage of innocence. To some people she is not reminiscent of any work of art. But she is really like a Tanagara statue, and would be rather annoyed if she were told so.' You can see just how witty and capricious she is in this speech which is touched with the absurd in its references, for instance, to the Achilles statue, the string trio and 'bimetallism'. The Tommy we hear about is a character who we never see, so Mabel's portrait of him must be vivid and deft. Notice how many times she uses the word 'propose'; for the best comic effect the word must have a different emphasis each time it is repeated. She has a great love of theatrical effects, and is just off to an amateur dramatic rehearsal. She wishes Tommy would be a bit more theatrical.

Mrs Warren's Profession
(1902) Bernard Shaw

Act 4. Honoria Fraser's chambers in Chancery Lane.

Vivie Warren is described by Shaw as 'an attractive specimen of the sensible, able, highly educated young middle-class Englishwoman. Age 22. Prompt, strong, confident, self-possessed.' She confronts her mother Mrs Warren with her decision to leave home. Vivie is unsentimental and rather cool to the news that her mother's past includes a life as a prostitute and more currently as a madam. These facts, however, prompt Vivie to seek a separate life of her own. The speech is part of a heated argument with her mother over whether she should marry Crofts, her mother's choice of husband for her.

VIVIE. . . .
Mother: you dont at all know the sort of person I am. I dont object to Crofts more than to any other coarsely built man of his class. To tell you the truth, I rather admire him for being strongminded enough to enjoy himself in his own way and make plenty of money instead of living the usual shooting, hunting, dining-out, tailoring, loafing life of his set merely because all the rest do it. And I'm perfectly aware that if I'd been in the same circumstances as my aunt Liz, I'd have done exactly what she did. I dont think I'm more prejudiced or straitlaced than you: I think I'm less. I'm certain I'm less sentimental. I know very well that fashionable morality is all a pretence, and that if I took your money and devoted the rest of my life to spending it fashionably, I might be as worthless and vicious as the silliest woman could possibly want to be without having a word said to me about it. But I dont want to be worthless. I shouldnt enjoy trotting about the park to advertise my dressmaker and carriage builder, or being bored at the opera to shew off a shopwindowful of diamonds.

Wait a moment: I'm not done . . . No: I am my mother's daughter. I am like you: I must have work, and must make more money than I spend. But my work is not your work, and my way not your way. We must part. It will not make much difference to us: instead of meeting one another for perhaps a few months in twenty years, we shall never meet: that's all.

COMMENTARY: Shaw's *Mrs Warren's Profession* caused a storm of outrage and protest when it was produced at the beginning of the century. Mrs Warren's profession is prostitution. She has kept this a secret from her daughter Vivie, who she has raised to be an educated and independent woman and who she would like to see take her place in proper society. There is much unsentimental description justifying Mrs Warren's life. The play ends, however, with Vivie's decision to leave her mother and strike out as a professional woman on her own. Shaw shows ironically the independent streak shared by mother and daughter even as their relationship deteriorates throughout the play and bitterness rises to the surface.

Vivie is the new breed of educated woman with a degree in mathematics from Cambridge University. Marriage and life in a vain and stupid society have no appeal for her. At the beginning of the play, she encapsulates her ambitions as follows: 'I shall set up in chambers in the City, and work at actuarial calculations and conveyancing. Under cover of that I shall do some law, with one eye on the Stock Exchange all the time. Ive come down here by myself to read law: not for a holiday, as my mother imagines. I hate holidays.' Vivie is passionately precise and approaches life as a mathematical equation. She likes smoking (even cigars), drinking and enjoys nothing better than an intellectual challenge. She is all mind; romance and marriage have no part in her highly organised scheme. Notice how brisk and clipped her sentences are. Her words are short on mournful vowels and favour sharp consonants. What she does here is lecture her mother on her view of life as she knows and has experienced it. She uses a lot of negative phrases; many no's and dont's. There is a fierceness to Vivie which the actor must not resist showing. This is her declaration of independence.

In the Shadow of the Glen
(1903) J M Synge

The kitchen in the last cottage at the head of a long glen in County Wicklow, Ireland.

Nora Burke (20s) sits in her cottage tending the shrouded corpse of her recently deceased husband. She is visited by her neighbour, the timid Michael Dara, and a strange poetic tramp who both stop by and pay their respects to the new widow. Michael Dara would like to be Nora's new suitor and begins to draw her out about her relationship with the dead Dan Burke. They are sitting at the table having cups of tea. The tramp is sleeping in the corner of the room.

NORA (*in a low voice*).
It was no lie you heard, Michael Dara . . . (*Giving him his tea.*) It's in a lonesome place you do have to be talking with someone, and looking for someone, in the evening of the day, and if it's a power of men I'm after knowing they were fine men, for I was a hard child to please, and a hard girl to please, (*She looks at him a little sternly.*) and it's a hard woman I am to please this day, Michael Dara, and it's no lie I'm telling you . . . What way would I live, and I an old woman, if I didn't marry a man with a bit of a farm, and cows on it and sheep on the back hills? . . . I do be thinking in the long nights it was a big fool I was that time, Michael Dara; for what good is a bit of a farm with cows on it, and sheep on the back hills, when you do be sitting looking out from a door the like of that door, and seeing nothing but the mists rolling down the bog, and the mists again and they rolling up the bog, and hearing nothing but the wind crying out in the bits of broken trees were left from the great storm, and the streams roaring with the rain. . . . It's a bad night, and a wild night Michael Dara, and isn't it a great

114

while I am at the foot of the back hills, sitting up here boiling food for himself, and food for the brood sow, and baking a cake when the night falls? Isn't it a long while I am sitting here in the winter and the summer, and the fine spring, with the young growing behind me and the old passing, saying to myself one time to look on Mary Brien, who wasn't that height (*Holding out her hand.*) and I a fine girl growing up, and there she is now with two children, and another coming on her in three months or four. (*Pauses.*) . . . And saying to myself another time, to look on Peggy Cavanagh, who had the lightest hand at milking a cow that wouldn't be easy, or turning a cake, and there she is now walking round on the roads, or sitting in a dirty old house, with no teeth in her mouth, and no sense, and no more hair than you'd see on a bit of hill and they after burning the furze on it. . . . Why would I marry you, Mike Dara? You'll be getting old and I'll be getting old, and in a little while, I'm telling you, you'll be sitting up in your bed – the way himself was sitting – with a shake in your face, and your teeth falling, and the white hair sticking out round you like an old bush where sheep do be leaping a gap. . . . It's a pitiful thing to be getting old, but it's a queer thing surely. It's a queer thing to see an old man sitting up there in his bed with no teeth in him, and a rough word in his mouth, and his chin the way it would take the bark from the edge of an oak board you'd have building a door . . . God forgive me, Michael Dara, we'll all be getting old, but it's a queer thing surely.

COMMENTARY: Synge's *In the Shadow of the Glen* is a one-act play based on a folktale about a jealous old husband who feigns death in order to test whether or not his wife will be instantly unfaithful. Dan Burke is lying under a sheet playing a corpse, while his wife Nora entertains two potential suitors who come to pay their respects. When Dan rises up finally and shows he is still alive, Nora suddenly realises that she has wasted her life being married to such a suspicious and jealous old fool and runs off with the lyrical tramp who has charmed her. She leaves behind the other suitor, Michael Dara, who seems more interested in money than in Nora.

Nora is a garrulous woman to whom torrents of words come naturally. Within the limits of her life, her own natural gift for poetry creates a vast expanse of space and freedom beyond her limited frame of reference. Her youth has been circumscribed by marriage and the boundaries of an isolated farm. Nora has only her imagination to retreat to. The last thing she wants is another husband who will constrain her in the same way. Notice the wonderful way her language rises and falls like the hills that surround her. She refers regularly to that landscape and what goes on there. Nora is a child of nature and wants to break the regimented routine of chores that hem her in. Although the speech is not written in dialect it does have colloquial intonations and rhythms which you naturally fall into once you start speaking. Let these rhythms do the work for you and do not artificially impose an Irish accent. She is speaking low and confidentially, trying to preserve reverence for the dead. Relish the word pictures and create them simply without force.

Major Barbara
(1907) Bernard Shaw

Act 3. The library of Lady Britomart's London town house in Wilton Crescent.

Barbara Undershaft, in Shaw's own description, is 'robust, jolly and energetic'. Up until and through the second act of the play she has been an enthusiastic and idealistic member of the Salvation Army. Her father Andrew Undershaft, a wealthy munitions dealer, has wounded her ideals and made her see the harsh social and economic realities of the everyday world. In this monologue she debates with her fiancé Adolphus Cusins (Dolly) about human nature, sin and suffering.

BARBARA.
There is no wicked side: life is all one. And I never wanted to shirk my share in whatever evil must be endured, whether it be sin or suffering. I wish I could cure you of middle-class ideas, Dolly. . . . That is why I have no class, Dolly: I come straight out of the heart of the whole people. If I were middle-class I should turn my back on my father's business; and we should both live in an artistic drawing room, with you reading the reviews in one corner, and I in the other at the piano, playing Schumann: both very superior persons, and neither of us a bit of use. Sooner than that, I would sweep out the guncotton shed, or be one of Bodger's barmaids. Do you know what would have happened if you had refused papa's offer? . . . I should have given you up and married the man who accepted it. After all, my dear old mother has more sense than any of you. I felt like her when I saw this place – felt that I must have it – that never, never, never could I let it go; only she thought it was the houses and the kitchen ranges and the linen and china, when it was really all the human souls to be saved: not weak souls in starved bodies, sobbing

117

with gratitude for a scrap of bread and treacle, but fullfed, quarrelsome, snobbish, uppish creatures, all standing on their little rights and dignities, and thinking that my father ought to be greatly obliged to them for making so much money for him – and so he ought. That is where salvation is really wanted. My father shall never throw it in my teeth again that my converts were bribed with bread. (*She is transfigured.*) I have got rid of the bribe of bread. I have got rid of the bribe of heaven. Let God's work be done for its own sake: the work he had to create us to do because it cannot be done except by living men and women. When I die, let him be in my debt, not I in his; and let me forgive him as becomes a woman of my rank.

COMMENTARY: *Major Barbara* concerns the conflict between opposing views on the 'right' ways to save the world. Barbara, a major in the Salvation Army, has left the comfortable confines of her upper-class home to wallow in the neglect and social deprivation of London's East End. She believes that men's souls can and should be saved and eventually realises that their stomachs need to be full before they can become converts. She learns this from her pragmatic father who rose from poor East End origins to become a wealthy munitions broker.

Barbara has returned home and forsaken her uniform for civilian dress. But one thing she cannot shed is the rhetoric of the true believer. She may no longer be as passionate about the poor as before but she can still become 'transfigured' by the thought of a classless society. At every point in the play Barbara tries to rise above her conditions and see the world from a fresh perspective. Shaw tends to give his characters pulpits from which to preach their beliefs. They don't so much talk as make eloquent pronouncements that read like a string of epigrams. Keeping the words alive and real for the actor is the central challenge of performing Shaw. Once the monologue becomes too didactic it is lost. Barbara appears here like a born-again Christian whose ardour has simply taken a new direction and subject. In the end she comes to espouse a curious mixture of spiritual *and* material values. She has all the strength and vision of a Saint Joan of Arc.

The Marriage
(1833) Nikolai Gogol

Act 2. St Petersburg. A room in Agafya Tikhonovna's house.

Agafya (26), the unmarried daughter of a merchant, is an expectant bride-to-be. A matchmaker has brought a number of prospective grooms to her house and she is trying to decide from among the assortment. She is talking to herself, trying to make up her mind.

AGAFYA.
Oh dear, oh dear what a mess I'm in. How will I ever make my choice? Now, if only there were one or two gentlemen – but there are four! I'll just have to decide between them. Mr Anutchkin isn't bad looking; but he is a bit on the skinny side. Mr Podkolyossin's not bad looking either. And Mr Omelet, well, he is rather fat, but he is still quite attractive. How am I going to sort this out? And then there's Mr Zhevakin, also a fine gentleman. Oh it's so difficult to make up my mind. Now, if I could put Anutchkin's lips with Podkolyossin's nose and add a touch of Zhevakin's confidence plus a bit of Omelet's girth, then I might be able to choose. It's just so confusing! Thinking about it's making my head throb . . . I've got it – I'll draw lots. In God's will I trust – which ever of them I pick, he'll be my husband. I'll write each of their names on a scrap of paper, screw it up tightly – and what will be, will be. (*Goes to her desk, takes scissors and paper, cuts out four lots, rolls them up and continues speaking.*) A girl's life can be pretty trying, especially when she's in love. Men just don't know what she's going through, they don't understand her feelings . . . That's it, everything's ready! I'll put them in my bag, close my eyes, and what will be, will be. (*She puts lots into her bag and*

shakes them up.) Oh this is so awful! . . . Dear God, please let it be Mr Anutchkin. No, why him? Let's have Mr Podkolyossin instead. But why him? What's the matter with the others then? . . . No, no . . . which ever one comes up, then he's the one. (*Fumbles inside her bag, and pulls out all the lots at once*.) Ohh . . . all of them! All of them! My heart's racing. No. One. One. I have to pick one. (*Puts lots back into her bag, shakes them up*.) Ohh, let it be Mr Zhevakin! . . . Oh dear, what am I saying? I meant to say Mr Anutchkin . . . No. No. Let fortune decide.

COMMENTARY: Gogol's *The Marriage* is a wonderful farce about matchmaking. A group of fantastical male suitors are brought to the home of the bride-to-be, Agafya Tikhonovna. She has to choose one from among them, as they all argue for and against marriage in their own strange ways. The comedy ends unexpectedly as one of the leading suitors, Podkolyossin, jumps out of the window and runs off when he is chosen as the lucky man. Gogol subtitled his play 'A Completely Unlikely Incident in Two Acts'.

All of Gogol's plays are full of comically grotesque characters. A few traits of each are exaggerated to huge proportions so that the character functions in relation to his or her queer behaviour. Agafya is a character who cannot make up her mind when faced with a choice. She is a bit old to be looking for a husband, in terms of her own society, and is probably getting a bit desperate. She finds it hard to speak in public, makes social gaffes repeatedly and is in a constant state of embarrassment. She has very little in the way of cultivated social graces. In this speech she looks at her suitors as if they were dolls with interchangeable parts. They have no personalities, only superficial features. She never mentions the word 'love' or anything more deeply spiritual. Notice how the pressure builds in the speech; her head is first throbbing and then her heart is racing; she is a nervous wreck. It is a wonderfully physical scene focused and contained through the scraps of paper which she manages to bungle. When we first see her in the play she is having her fortune read and here she leaves the choice up to fortune. As she says, 'what will be, will be'. In all of Gogol's writing life is a gamble.

Woyzeck

(1836–7) Georg Büchner

Scenes 4 & 18. Marie's room.

Marie (20s) is a poor lower-class woman who is Woyzeck's common-law wife. Together they have a child. In an earlier scene she has become infatuated with a virile Drum Major who has given her a pair of earrings and is in the process of seducing her. In a later scene the affair has gone horribly wrong and the rising tension gives her premonitions of dire things to come. She turns to the Bible for comfort and tries to pray.

MARIE (*she is tucking the baby into its crib*).
The man gives him an order and he has to go, just like that. (*She takes a piece of broken mirror from her blouse and examines the earrings she is wearing.*) Look how they catch the light. I wonder what they are? What'd he say? – Go to sleep, baby, shut your eyes tight. (*She bends over towards the crib.*) Tighter. That's it. Now you keep still or else he'll come and get you.
(*Sings.*) Polly, close the shutter tight,

      A gipsy lad will come tonight.

      He will take you by the hand

      And lead you off to gipsy land.

– They must be gold! An old crack in the back wall of a corner to live in and a bit of broken glass to see with, that's enough for the likes of us. My mouth's as red as my lady's, though, for all her full-length mirrors and rows of fine gentlemen kissing her hand. An' I'm just another poor girl – Sshh, baby, close your eyes. (*She oscillates the fragment.*) Here comes the sandman, walking across the wall. Keep your eyes closed! If he looks in them you'll go blind.

Woyzeck enters. Marie starts and covers her ears.

The child is in its crib, Marie kneels nearby with an open Bible.

'. . . Neither was guile found in his mouth.' Don't look at me, Lord. (*She turns to another page.*) 'And the scribes and the pharisees brought unto him a woman taken in adultery, and set her in the midst . . . And Jesus said unto her, "Neither do I condemn thee. Go, and sin no more."' (*Tries to hold her hands together in prayer.*) I can't. – Can't. Dear God, don't take everything, at least let me pray. (*The child stirs and she comforts him.*) And Frantz doesn't come. Yesterday, today. Still doesn't come. – It gets so hot! (*Goes to the window and opens it, comes back to the Bible. She picks it up and reads where she's standing.*) ' . . . And she stood at his feet behind him weeping, and began to wash his feet with tears and did wipe them with the hairs of her head, and kissed his feet and anointed them with an ointment.' (*Strikes herself on the breast.*) Dead; all dead! – Oh my Lord, my Lord! If only I could anoint your feet.

Translated by John Mackendrick

COMMENTARY: Büchner's *Woyzeck* is a tragedy that was written in 1836, but not published until 1879, nor performed until 1913. The script was left in unordered fragments at the author's death (at the age of 23) and so there is no definitive version of the play. Büchner based the drama on the actual murder case of a barber who stabbed his mistress in a fit of jealousy and was then sentenced to death. The playwright adds to the drama by showing that other psychic forces are at work on Woyzeck (like class, science, environment, atmosphere and religion), leading him to distraction as he commits a crime he does not want to commit. Woyzeck, though a good man, is used and manipulated by everyone in the play. His sense of identity and self whittles away to nothing. Marie, his common-law wife, plays a vital part in Woyzeck's downfall. The play radically influenced both naturalist and expressionist drama.

Marie's speech, like the play itself, is loaded with fragments and telegraphed thoughts. Her first scene is eager and uplifting with the mirror and earrings, setting a tone of newly awakened vanity. The later scene is more brooding and religious, taking its tone from the biblical tale of Mary Magdalene. Both scenes are like little moral sketches. The actor in both instances must perform two actions at once: caring for the child and performning the main action of the scene. There is a constant back-and-forth motion from crib to mirror or Bible. Marie is an instinctive mother easily distracted by the child's interruptions. She is not overtly intelligent so her monologue is really a series of voiced thoughts. It is up to the actor to give the scenes shape and purpose. Marie implies more than she expresses since her simplicity means that she does not use many words. Notice how full of action both scenes are: caring, singing, reading, looking, listening, passing time alone. Literally half the scene is acted out in silence with the words punctuating movement. Marie has a vivid interior life that switches from gold to God and these subjects focus her thoughts. The actor has to create a sense of enclosure and protectiveness which Woyzeck invades at the end of the first scene. These are both very private moments, more full of musings than declarative speeches.

A Month in the Country
(1850) Ivan Turgenev

Act 4. A large unfurnished outer room in a house on a Russian
country estate. Summer.

*Natalya Petrovna (29) is married to a wealthy landowner. She has a
son Kolya who is ten years old and a stepdaughter Vera who is
seventeen. She is bored with her stuffy, dull husband and with her
restrictive provincial life. She has fallen in love with her son's tutor
Alexey Nikolayevitch Belyaev, a twenty-one-year-old student. She
thinks he is in love with Vera and has schemed first to dismiss Belyaev
and then to get rid of her rival. However, Belyaev has just told Vera
that he only loves her as a sister. Now Natalya makes her confession.*

NATALYA PETROVNA.

Wait, Alexey Nikolayevitch . . . The truth is . . . Vera is
right . . . It's time I . . . time for me to end all this lying.
I've done an injustice to her and to you too. You've every
right to despise me. (*Belyaev makes an involuntary gesture.*)
In my own eyes I've degraded myself. I've only one way to
win back your respect: honesty, absolute honesty, whatever
the consequences. And what's more I'm seeing you here for
the last time, speaking to you for the last time. I love you.
(*She continues, but does not look at him.*) . . . Yes, oh yes, I
love you. Vera wasn't deceiving herself, she hasn't deceived
you either. I've loved you from the first day you came here,
but I only realised this yesterday. I'm not going to attempt
to justify what I've done. It was inexcusable . . . And now,
at least, you can understand, understand, and forgive. Yes,
I was jealous of Vera; yes, I was scheming to marry her off
to Bolshintsov, to get her away from me and from you; yes,
I took advantage of my position, of my age, to discover her
secret – and of course I didn't reckon on this – I gave myself

away in the process. I love you, Belyaev; but you've got to understand it's only pride that pushes me to confess this . . . This farce I've been performing has finally disgusted me. You can't remain here . . . In fact, after what I've just told you, you'll probably feel very ill at ease around me, and you'll want to be gone from here as quickly as you can. That much I feel certain about. And that certainty has given me courage. Of course I don't want you to think badly of me. Now you know all there is to know . . . maybe I've spoilt it for you . . . maybe if this hadn't all happened you might have fallen in love with Vera . . . I've only got one explanation to offer you, Alexey Nikolayevitch . . . It's all been beyond my control. (*She pauses. She has said all of this in a calm and measured voice, not looking at Belyaev. He says nothing. She continues with some agitation, still not looking at him.*) You don't answer me? But I understand that. There's nothing you can say to me. The situation of a man receiving a declaration of love when he feels no love – it's just too painful. I thank you for your silence. Believe me, when I told you . . . that I love you, it wasn't make-believe . . . like before; I wasn't taking anything for granted, in fact, the opposite was true; I wanted to throw away that mask which, I can tell you, I'm not used to wearing . . . And in any case, what's the point of affectation and pretence, when everything's out in the open; why make-believe when there's no one left to deceive? It's all over between us now. I won't keep you. You can go. You don't have to say another word to me, not even goodbye. I won't take it as lack of courtesy, instead I'll be grateful. A situation like this doesn't call for delicacy . . . in this case it would be quite inappropriate. It appears that we weren't destined to know one another any better . . . So, goodbye! Yes, we just weren't destined to know each other . . . and at least now I hope you won't see me any longer as some kind of secretive, deceitful tyrant . . . Goodbye for ever.

COMMENTARY: Turgenev's *A Month in the Country* is a bitter-sweet comedy that focuses on the romantic entanglements that disrupt the routine harmony of life on a country estate. Natalya Petrovna, the wife of the estate owner, Islayev, falls in love with her son's young tutor. The affair is complicated by the fact that she thinks she has a rival in Vera, her seventeen-year-old stepdaughter. A family friend, Rakitin, a frequent visitor to the estate, is in love with Natalya, adding another level of complication. All of this is brought to a climax when the tutor reveals that he too loves Natalya and not Vera. The play ends with everyone left heartbroken, but wiser.

Natalya's speech is an avalanche of embarrassed and contradictory emotions. She is declaring her love to a younger man and it takes a bit of time to sort it all out into a speech. She is really thinking out loud, and needs to order her emotions into words. Belyaev cannot even get a word in edgeways. On different levels she indulges in self-recriminations, confessions and aggressive admissions. A myriad of emotions are in play at the same time, warring with and contradicting one another. As she says it is all beyond her control. The actor must prevent herself from playing this too melodramatically. It is tempting to go in that direction; however, if you play against the melodrama, and observe Turgenev's stage directions, you get a much more truthful layer of character. Notice how she avoids looking at Belyaev for most of the speech. It would help too if you see the character's predicament as slightly ridiculous, for that is how Natalya views it herself.

The Storm
(1860) Alexander Ostrovsky

Act 5. Russia. A public garden high on the banks of the Volga. Twilight.

Katerina Kabanova (20s) is married to an ineffectual husband with an overbearing mother. Katerina finds her life repressive and lacking in spontaneous joy. Through religion she experiences an almost mystical escape, and her thoughts often turn to death and suicide. She dreams of escaping with a fantasy lover. She is drawn into an adulterous affair with Boris, a young well-educated man, while her husband is out of town. Once their ten-day affair is discovered guilt preys on her and she becomes increasingly despondent and desperate. She is walking along the riverbank practically in a state of delirium.

KATERINA (*she speaks as if in a trance, barely aware of what she is saying*).

No, I can't find him anywhere. My poor darling, what can you be doing now? I just want to say good-bye to you. Then . . . then, I might as well die. Why did I get him into trouble? It didn't make things any easier for me! It's me alone who should suffer! But I've ruined my life, and I've ruined his. I've disgraced myself and humiliated him for ever. (*Silence.*) Now just what was it he said to me? What were those words he used? (*Holds her head.*) I can't remember. I've forgotten it all. At night – at night, my suffering is worst. They all go off to bed – me too, they sleep easily – but it's as if I'm in my grave. The darkness is so terrible! I can hear such strange noises – like the singing at a funeral, but it's so soft that I can barely hear it – like it's far away . . . When it gets light again I'm so happy! But I can't stand getting up; I can't stand seeing the same faces, hearing the same conversations, going through the same torment, again and again. Why do they look at me like that? Why don't they kill unfaithful wives any more? Why is it all different now? In the old days, so they say, people would've killed you. They'd have taken me to the Volga and thrown me in. And if they did that I'd have been so glad. Ah, they say, if you were put to death, your sin would be forgiven. But haven't I suffered enough already? How much longer can this torment go on? What have I got to live for now, in any case? There's nothing I want, there's nothing I care for any more. But death, it just doesn't come. You pray for it, still it doesn't come. Everything I see, everything I hear just increases my pain, right here. (*Pressing her heart.*) If only I could live with him. I might have some happiness . . . What difference would that make now, anyhow? My soul is already damned. Oh, I miss you so terribly, I long to see you! And even though I can't see you, just hear me from afar! Oh let the wild winds carry my sorrow and pain to you! O God – it's so depressing, it's so depressing. (*Goes to the riverbank and shouts loudly.*) Darling. My joy. Life of my heart, my soul – I love you. Please, answer me! (*Bursts out crying.*)

COMMENTARY: Ostrovsky's *The Storm* is a tragic drama set in a claustrophobic provincial town on the banks of the Volga river. It is the study of the harsh life of a lower-class mercantile family that is ruled by a domineering matriarch. Marfa Kabanova dominates her son Tikhon and daughter-in-law Katerina with an iron will. Katerina's sensitivity and mysticism seek freedom in an affair with the attractive and educated Boris but her guilt consumes her and she confesses publicly that she is an adulteress. After scenes of self-castigation she finally ends her life by flinging herself into the Volga during a violent thunderstorm.

Katerina's free spirit and will are crushed by tragedy. She lives an oppressed life and vainly searches for freedom and air that will allow her to breathe. It is a mistake to play her as a melodramatic heroine. Her entire being is sensitive; her head pounds, blood rushes through her veins. She experiences everything viscerally. Every assault is an attack on her senses. Notice how the speech exerts enormous pressure on her, forcing her to cry out as a means of release. This is the climactic point in the speech where words no longer serve a purpose. Notice too that she is entirely alone, hemmed in and cut off. She is consumed by neurotic agitation and is in severe pain, grieving that her lover has been taken from her. This is not a speech you can attempt without a good deal of internal preparation, conviction and control. Oddly enough the pain is a kind of welcomed relief for Katerina. It finally allows her to open up.

A Doll's House
(1879) Henrik Ibsen

Act 3. Norway. A room furnished not expensively, but comfortably and tastefully. It is evening.

Nora (20s–30s) has been married to Torvald Helmer, a successful lawyer and bank manager, for eight years. He has kept her pampered, protected and isolated at home. He treats her like a child, giving her the nickname 'Little Squirrel'. However, Nora, having forged her father's signature on a cheque to get the money to pay for a life-saving holiday for her husband, is now being threatened with blackmail by the moneylender Nils Krogstad. This evening the couple have been to a party where Helmer consumed a lot of champagne. After coming home Helmer opens a letter from Krogstad threatening that the only way to avoid a scandal is if Helmer creates a position for Krogstad at his bank. When Helmer confronts Nora with this letter, and fails to appreciate her motives in all this, she starts to realise that her marriage is merely a sham.

NORA.

You've never really loved me. You just thought it was fun to be in love with me – that's all . . . It's true Torvald. When I lived at home with papa, he would tell me what he thought about everything, so I never had any opinions of my own. And if I ever had any ideas of my own I made sure to keep them absolutely secret and hidden, because he wouldn't have wanted it any other way. He used to call me his little doll, and he'd play with me just as I played with my own dolls. Then I came to live with you in your house . . . What I mean is, that I passed directly from papa's hands into yours. You've always arranged things just so, the way you wanted them, and I simply adopted the very same tastes as yours – well, at least I pretended I did – I can't quite remember – Anyway, I suppose it was a bit of both really – first one – then the other. But now, looking back, it's as if I were a beggar living here – from hand to mouth. I survived by performing tricks for you, Torvald. But that's the way you preferred it. You know it's a terrible wrong that you and papa have done me. It's your fault that I've made nothing of my life. . . . Our home's been nothing but a play-pen. I've been your doll-wife, just as I was papa's doll-child. And then in their turn the children have been my dolls. I used to think that it was fun when you'd come in and play with me, just as the children think it's fun when I go in and play with them. But that, Torvald, is all that our marriage amounts to.

COMMENTARY: Ibsen's *A Doll's House* uses elements of the problem play with intrigue and some melodrama to probe a marriage that is based on false premises. The image of a wife trapped in a marriage has had a resonant influence down through the decades. Nora's selfless act to aid her husband is greeted by his harsh and unremitting anger. On the basis of that reaction, Nora leaves Helmer and her children, with the famous slamming of the door, to seek a life in which she can be more than just a plaything.

Nora's recognition speech brings to the surface all of her pent-up frustration and resentment. The scales drop from her eyes and she sees the truth for the first time. Her husband has kept her in domestic bondage and servitude. Her life has been inextricably linked to his, and has no independence apart from him. Notice that her suppression by men stretched back to her 'papa'. Even Krogstad the blackmailer uses her. There has been a pattern of suppression in every part of her life. The other thing Nora now resents is the frivolity and child-like existence she has been maintaining. Part of Nora's problem is that she has never had the room to mature. She has been a daddy's girl and has stayed that way until this moment. The actor should realise that Nora has never had a confrontational moment until now. Whatever resentment she may have had in the past was never openly voiced. There might be a bit of tentativeness as you start out on this monologue until you finally find the freedom – and confidence – that the speech offers you.

Miss Julie
(1888) August Strindberg

A large kitchen in a Swedish country house. Midsummer eve.

Miss Julie (25) is the daughter of a Count. Jean (30) is her father's valet who is engaged to Kristin the cook. Jean is confident, ambitious and intelligent and dreams of moving up in the world. In his eyes, Miss Julie is the incarnation of all he aspires to. Miss Julie is listless, bored and frustrated and she amuses herself by dallying with the servants on her father's estate while he is away. During the Midsummer celebrations Miss Julie visits the kitchen. She and Jean engage in seductive, provocative chat, which, like a game of cat and mouse, leads to a violent off-stage sexual encounter. Jean wants to use her to rise above his class. They rashly plan to run away together to Switzerland to start a new life. When Miss Julie wants to bring her pet canary with her, Jean says no and she defies him by saying 'kill it or kill me'. He impulsively grabs the canary and in front of Miss Julie cuts its head off on the chopping board.

MISS JULIE.
Kill me! Kill me too! You, who can kill such a tiny, innocent creature. And your hand didn't even tremble! Oh how I hate you, how I despise you! Now there's blood between us. I curse the moment I first saw you. I curse the moment I was conceived in my mother's womb. (*She approaches the chopping board as if drawn to it against her will.*) No, I won't go yet. I can't . . . I've got to see . . . Shh! There's a carriage coming. (*She listens, but keeps her eyes fastened on the chopping board.*) You think I can't stand the sight of blood, don't you? You think I'm so weak. Oh I'd love to see your blood – your brain – there on that chopping board. I'd love to see the whole of your sex swimming in its own blood just like my little bird! I feel I

could drink out of your skull, bathe in your broken chest, and devour your roasted heart. – You think I'm weak! You think I love you, that my womb yearns for your seed, that I want to carry your child under my heart, feeding it with my blood. Bear your child! Take your name! Oh now just a moment . . . what is your name, anyway? I've never heard your last name. I suppose you don't have one, do you . . . I'd be 'Mrs Hovel' or 'Madam Dunghill'. You dog, you, sporting my collar – you valet with my crest on your buttons! You think I'm going to share you with my cook – have that servant as my rival! Oh! Oh! Oh! . . . You think I'm a coward and I'll just run away. No. I'm staying put – come what may. My father will come back . . . find his desk broken into . . . his money gone. Then he'll ring that bell – the usual two rings, Jean . . . for his valet . . . he'll send for the police . . . and then . . . I shall tell him the whole story. Every single, little detail! Oh it'll be wonderful to have it over and done with . . . if only it will be over . . . Then he'll have a stroke and die. That will be the sad end of our family. There will just be peace and quiet . . . for ever and ever. The family coat of arms will be broken over his coffin – the noble line extinguished. But the valet's line continues on in the orphanage, wins glory in the gutter and ends in jail.

COMMENTARY: Strindberg's *Miss Julie* is a long one-act tragedy which charts the rise and fall of a one-night relationship between the aristocratic Miss Julie and her father's ambitious valet Jean. Their initial seduction and lovemaking eventually turns to quarrels and a brutal falling-out. The play culminates with Miss Julie leaving the stage to commit suicide and Jean left on-stage to face the returning Count, Julie's father. Two opposing poles are used to frame the action: master versus servant, upper versus lower class, night versus day, love versus hate, affection versus lust, and man versus woman. In Strindberg's world the conflict between the sexes is the most critical one of all and he pits two formidable antagonists against each other.

Throughout the play Julie has shown increasing signs of instability. She is uneasy about herself and her identity and what her role should be in life. She flirts with danger and in the person of Jean it has finally caught her in its grips. She has been degraded in the course of the play, has confessed her innermost thoughts and secrets, has had her virginity ruthlessly taken from her and has permitted herself to be ordered about by her own servant. All these reversals are now reaching an emotional climax in the final moments of the play. The sight of blood gives Julie her final shock of recognition. From this moment on her thoughts turn to revenge and suicide. Notice how she focuses on the dead canary and literally begins transforming into another person. The blood has a strong effect on her. Her anger builds and builds along with her disgust. The entire speech is a series of fragments. Julie is at her wits' end, suffering disconnections and disassociations on every level. Lurid sexual images (i.e. castration) feed her vengefulness as the savage speech becomes one huge apocalyptic rant.

The Seagull
(1896) Anton Chekhov

Act 4. A reception room of a Russian country estate. A dark and stormy night in autumn.

Nina (18–20s), the daughter of a wealthy landowner, fled her protective country home to become an actress. Two years earlier on this same estate she fell in love with Trigorin, a famous older novelist, who encouraged her to follow him to Moscow. Her next-door neighbour in the country, Konstantin, the writer son of the renowned actress Madame Arkadina (who also loves Trigorin) had been in love with Nina and featured her in his first play. In this scene Nina, having secretly returned from a harsh existence as a lowly provincial actress and afraid to go home, reveals herself to Konstantin (Kostya). This prompts him to declare his undiminished love and adoration for her. During her two-year absence Nina not only became an actress but had an illegitimate child by Trigorin which subsequently died. She is exhausted, disoriented and bitter. During the speech she discovers that Trigorin is in the next room.

NINA.
Why do you say you kiss the ground I walk on? I should be destroyed. (*Leaning on a table.*) I'm so tired! If only I could rest . . . rest! (*Raising her head.*) I am the seagull . . . No, that's not it. I am an actress. Yes! (*Hearing Mme Arkadina and Trigorin laughing, she listens, then runs to the door and looks through the keyhole.*) So, he's here too . . . (*Going to Konstantin.*) Yes, of course . . . It doesn't matter . . . He didn't believe in the theatre, he would always laugh at my dreams – and little by little, I stopped believing too. I just lost heart. Then, on top of everything came the strain of love, the jealousy, the endless anxiety for my baby. . . . I became petty and superficial. My acting lost all focus. I didn't know what to do with my hands, I didn't know how

to stand on stage. I couldn't control my voice. You can't imagine what it feels like when you know you're acting badly. I am the seagull. No, that's not it . . . Do you remember, you shot a seagull? One day quite by chance, a man came by there, he sees it, and because he had nothing better to do, he destroys it . . . It's an idea for a short story . . . No, that's not it . . . (*Rubbing her forehead.*) What was I saying? About the theatre. Yes. I'm not like that now. I'm a real actress. I act with joy, with rapture. On stage it's as if I'm intoxicated – I perform magnificently. And since I've arrived here, I keep walking about and thinking and thinking, and feeling that each day my spiritual strength is growing . . . Now I know, Kostya, now I understand, that in our calling – whether it's acting or writing – the essential thing – what really matters – is not the fame, not the glory, none of those things I used to dream of – it's knowing how to endure. To bear one's cross – to keep faith. I have faith and things don't hurt so much any more. And when I think of my vocation, I stop fearing life.

COMMENTARY: *The Seagull* is partly about the ambitions of a young would-be actress Nina and a burgeoning writer Konstantin, to flee their isolation and loneliness in order to establish themselves as individuals and artists in their own right. Though in love at the beginning of the play when Nina first gets a taste of the stage as an actress, circumstances and other characters drive them apart until they are reunited in this final act. Both have changed irreparably during the two-year interval. Nina has learned to endure through hardship and accept her bitter fate while Konstantin suffers from a frustration that only deepens and leads to suicide.

By creating an ingenious series of interlocking triangular relationships and sudden shifts in mood, and by having them talk obsessively about someone else, Chekhov always increases the tensions and frustrations between his characters. Nina cannot talk to Konstantin without constantly referring to her shattered relationship with the writer Trigorin who first used and then abandoned her in Moscow. The infant from that union died. Two years earlier, in a fit of jealousy, Konstantin shot a seagull and laid it at Nina's feet. Trigorin then used that image in a story and Nina picks it up again here, attaching it to herself. The web of associations between past and present, fiction and reality circulate through Nina's mind as she delivers a monologue that loses its thread and then picks it up again. The actor must remember that Nina has a shadowy background and seems almost to appear out of the woods like a frightened, wounded bird. Her furtiveness is evident from the moment she enters and restlessly searches the room. The transformation in her looks is shocking. She has barely slept and looks haggard. Her dreams to be a great actress like Konstantin's mother Madame Arkadina have proven to be a delusion; she is just a modestly talented actress who tours the provinces, yet she still shows a strong belief in herself and that keeps her going. What she has learned most of all is how to endure and accept her fate. Every performer has to decide how she will play Nina's distracted state. How naïvely or ironically is she likening herself to a seagull? Is she going mad during the scene or maybe finally discovering herself and gaining health? The best performances of the part always accentuate the character's positive renewal of strength.

Uncle Vanya
(1899) Anton Chekhov

Act 3. A drawing-room of a Russian country house. Daytime.

Yelena (27) is married to a retired professor who is elderly, gout-ridden and pompous. She is spirited and beautiful although drowning in lethargy and boredom from having no purpose in life. Sonia, her stepdaughter, has just confided to her that she has been in love for the past six years with the local doctor Astrov, who barely seems to notice her. After revealing her secret Sonia leaves the stage.

YELENA *(alone).*

There's nothing worse than knowing somebody's secret and not being able to help them. *(Musing.)* He's not in love with her – that's obvious. But why doesn't he marry her? She's not beautiful, but for a country doctor, of his age, she'd make an excellent wife. She's intelligent, so good and so kind . . . No, that's not the point . . . *(Pause.)* I understand that poor girl. The desperate boredom here . . . Instead of real people she's surrounded by restless grey shadows, who do nothing but eat, drink, sleep and talk in stupid clichés. Then he makes one of his occasional appearances – he's not like the others, he's handsome, he's interesting, he's fascinating, like a bright moon rising in a dark night . . . To surrender to the charms of a man like that, forgetting oneself . . . I think I'm a bit fascinated too. Yes, when he's not here I'm bored – and now here I am smiling just thinking of him . . . Uncle Vanya says I have mermaid's blood in my veins, 'For once in your life let yourself go . . .' So, perhaps that's what I should do . . . Fly away from all of you like a free bird, away from all your sleepy faces and from all your chatter – to forget that you even exist . . . But I'm a coward, I'm shy . . . My conscience would catch me . . . He comes here, every day, I can guess why he comes, and already I feel guilty, ready to fall on my knees before Sonia, begging her forgiveness and weeping . . .

COMMENTARY: Chekhov's *Uncle Vanya* is a comedy that explores the dejection and disillusionment of a whole host of characters who come together on a country estate. Vanya has been managing the estate for his brother-in-law Professor Serebryakov, who take the profits and leaves nothing in return. Vanya's resentment is complicated by the infatuation he feels for the professor's young, beautiful wife Yelena. In fact, all of the men in the play, including the rational Dr Astrov, are attracted to her languorous charms and all of the women are in her shadow. Tensions reach a head when Vanya tries to shoot the professor. The status quo is uneasily restored at the end of the play as the professor and Yelena depart the scene, leaving Vanya and his niece Sonia behind, resigned to endure their lot.

Yelena is the catalyst for all the wild emotions that erupt during the course of the play. Whenever she is present characters reveal themselves and confess their innermost passions and loves. You will notice, however, that she is not a particularly sympathetic character nor does she offer a good shoulder to cry on. If anything she is a rival. She is quite remote and keeps her distance from everyone else's plight. She never lets herself go except when she shows romantic inclinations towards Dr Astrov; then we see a spark of romantic life. Her youth has been wasted in marriage to a pedantic old man. Notice how she tries to take flight in her speech, but remains mostly earthbound. She only flirts with letting herself go. She is fascinated by Sonia's emotional outburst and understands her desperation all too well. But Yelena has no programme or ambitions of her own. She cannot think beyond the very next moment. All the other characters imbue her with a mystique which she neither has nor deserves.

The Dance of Death
(1900) August Strindberg

Part II. Act 1, scene 1. Sweden. An oval drawing-room decorated in white and gold.

Alice (40s) lives with her husband, a retired commanding officer, in the military fortress which was once his base. The fortress is a circular tower on an island off the coast of Sweden which has become their 'Little Hell'. Over the years their relationship has deteriorated into an endless round of bitter acrimony and resentful quarrels. They hate rather than love. Every encounter between them is a chance to settle scores in their on-going marital battle. Allan, Alice's nephew, has come to live with them so that he can study with the Captain. He has fallen in love with Alice's daughter Judith, a 'coquette in pigtails', who teasingly flirts and taunts him. Allan has just run into the room crying while Alice is writing a letter. She tries to comfort him.

ALICE (*gentle, feminine, concerned*).
Don't be afraid of me, Allan. There's nothing to fear from me. What's the matter? Are you ill? . . . Do you have a headache? . . . (*Touches her breast.*) Is it here, in your heart? . . . A pain gnawing at your heart? Tearing it bit by bit . . . So that all you want is to die, you wish you were dead. Every tiny thing becomes so trying. There's only one thing on your mind – one person – but if it's two people, both thinking about the same person, then it's certain misery for one of them. (*Allan forgetting himself, fingers one of Judith's lace handkerchiefs which he found in the garden.*) It's a sickness that nobody can cure . . . You can't eat, you don't want to drink; you only want to weep – bitterly weep alone in the woods where no one can see you, far away from those who'd laugh at your grief. People can be so cruel. (*Shudders.*) What is it that you want from her? Nothing.
140

You don't want to kiss her on the lips, if you did that, you're sure that you'd just die. As your thoughts fly to her you feel as if death were creeping up on you. And it is death, my child – a death which gives life. But you can't understand that just yet . . . I can smell violets. It's her scent. (*Goes to Allan and gently takes away the handkerchief.*) There, there. Go on cry, yes, cry! That'll help to ease your heart. (*Pauses.*) Come on now, Allan, get up, be a man, if you don't, she won't want to look at you. The cruel girl, who is not cruel. Has she been tormenting you? With the Lieutenant. Listen, my boy. You must make friends with the Lieutenant, then you'll be able to talk together about her. That should help a bit.

COMMENTARY: Strindberg's *The Dance of Death* is a two-part play that works like a tragicomedy. It shifts abruptly from mood to mood (often within a single speech) and the actor must be prepared to go in whatever direction the author chooses. A character taunts when you expect them to comfort. Strindberg conceived the play as a claustrophobic battleground in which his celebrated war between the sexes could be played out in splendid isolation. In Part Two of the drama a young couple is introduced to serve as an antidote to the hostile relationship between Edgar and Alice.

Alice's speech is full of quirks and rapid shifts. She is both provoking and ministering simultaneously, both motherly and seductive. She promises and denies. She seems to be trying to make Allan feel worse, rather than better. Remember that she is talking about her own daughter, which makes some of the things she says sound hostile. When you play her you have to be kind and cruel in the same manipulative breath. Alice is a former actress and knows how to play a scene. She has also had years of experience tormenting and playing games with her husband. Allan is a new victim and she cannot put aside the habitual reactions of a lifetime in order to be genuine with him. You might want to consider how much of her own plight Alice sees in Allan's anguish. Both of them are at the mercy of volatile and petulant characters. Although a manipulator, you must keep that side of Alice perfectly balanced with her honest maternal instincts. Play her neither as a caricature nor a villain, and by all means do not judge her harshly. Play the balance and the tensions that are an essential part of the character.

Play Sources

Agamemnon by Aeschylus in *Aeschylus Plays: Two* (Methuen)

Antigone by Sophocles in *Sophocles: The Theban Plays* (Methuen)

Arden of Feversham, Anonymous in *Arden of Feversham* (New Mermaids)

As You Like It by William Shakespeare (various editions)

The Beaux' Stratagem by George Farquhar (New Mermaids)

The Changeling by Thomas Middleton & William Rowley in *Three Jacobean Tragedies* (Penguin)

The Country Wife by William Wycherley in *Three Restoration Comedies* (Penguin)

The Dance of Death by August Strindberg in *Strindberg Plays: Two* (Methuen)

A Doll's House by Henrik Ibsen in *Ibsen Plays: Two* (Methuen)

The Duchess of Malfi by John Webster in *John Webster: Three Plays* (Penguin)

Electra by Sophocles in *Sophocles Plays: Two* (Methuen)

The Game of Love and Chance by Pierre Marivaux in *Landmarks of French Classical Drama* (Methuen)

The Honest Whore (Part 1) by Thomas Dekker in *Dramatic Work: Thomas Dekker* (three volumes) (Cambridge University Press)

An Ideal Husband by Oscar Wilde in *Wilde: The Complete Plays* (Methuen)

In the Shadow of the Glen by J M Synge in *Synge: The Complete Plays* (Methuen)

Lady Windermere's Fan by Oscar Wilde in *Wilde: The Complete Plays* (Methuen)

Life is a Dream by Pedro Calderón de la Barca in *Calderón Plays: One* (Methuen)

The Lucky Chance by Aphra Behn in *Behn: Five Plays* (Methuen)

The Maid's Tragedy by Francis Beaumont & John Fletcher (Manchester University Press)

Major Barbara by Bernard Shaw (Penguin)

A Woman of No Importance by Oscar Wilde in *Wilde: The Complete Plays* (Methuen)

Women Beware Women by Thomas Middleton in *Thomas Middleton: Five Plays* (Penguin)

Woyzeck by Georg Büchner in *Büchner: The Complete Plays* (Methuen)